WOMEN
HAVING
IMPACT

FIELDING
UNIVERSITY PRESS

Fielding University Press is an imprint of Fielding Graduate University.
Its objective is to advance the research and scholarship of Fielding faculty,
students and alumni around the world, using a variety of publishing platforms.

For more information, please contact Fielding University Press, attention
Dr. Jean-Pierre Isbouts, via email to jisbouts@fielding.edu, or via postal mail to
Fielding Graduate University, 2020 De la Vina Street, Santa Barbara, CA 93105. On
the web at www.fielding.edu/universitypress.

Library of Congress Cataloging-in-Publication data
Women Having Impact
1.   Social Sciences – Education Leadership

WOMEN
HAVING
IMPACT

*How women of color are making a difference
in STEM at minority serving institutions*

Edited by

Kimarie Engerman

Tamara Floyd Smith

and

Stephanie Luster-Teasley

with a foreword by

Orlando Taylor

This book is dedicated to future Women Leaders of Color in STEM and the OURS (Opportunities for UnderRepresented Scholars) Leadership Team.

Table of Contents

FOREWORD

by Orlando L. Taylor, PhD

Vice President for Strategic Initiatives & Research
and Executive Director,
Center for the Advancement of STEM Leadership,
Fielding Graduate University

The STEM (science, technology, engineering and mathematic) fields will drive economies worldwide in the foreseeable future. Yet, women continue to be significantly underrepresented in most STEM disciplines worldwide – and women of color are more underrepresented than white women! These discrepancies are particularly alarming in the United States when one recognizes that women make up more than 60% of the nation's total student population and within African Americans, for example, close to 70%.

Because of the interrelationship between the robustness of the STEM workforce and a nation's potential for global competiveness, no nation can afford to limit access and equity for any demographic group. It is fair to say, therefore, that the United States will be unable to retain its global leadership in STEM over the long haul unless it becomes much more successful in broadening the participation of women generally and women of color in particular into the STEM disciplines.

After more than forty years of national attention to gender underrepresentation in STEM, access and equity remain an issue in the United States. Remedies for addressing the issue have rarely focused on preparing and advancing women into academic leadership roles in higher education. Yet, anecdotal evidence suggests that women academic leaders tend to produce more access, achievement and retention of women students in STEM.

Moreover, there is good evidence to suggest that strong organizations both inside and outside academia are intentional, and often formal, about preparing future leaders. In general, such preparation has NOT been the norm for STEM academic units, especially for women of color.

This book is a sequel to an earlier volume, entitled *Women Called to Lead*. That book focused more on the personal leadership journeys of several women who had participated in an NSF-funded academic leadership certificate program at The Chicago School of Professional Psychology and later at Fielding Graduate University. That program known as OURS (Opportunities for Underrepresented Scholars) has produced 55 women from HBCUs and Tribal Colleges from a variety of STEM fields, including the social, behavioral and economic sciences.

The focus of this current volume focuses on the experiences and successes of another group women, many of whom were also OURS completers. These authors describe how they have used the knowledge they have gained from leadership development and other experiences to impact their minority serving institution campuses to advance broadening participation of women (and men) in STEM at all levels from students to faculty and administration. In doing so, their essays provide a strong resource for women of color and women at all institutions. They are particularly useful for addressing the "no-gain/no-win" situation that many women academics find themselves as a result of their engagement in service-orientated activities without receiving the appropriate benefits or titles for the work done. In addition, several campus transformation initiatives led by women of color are described that have changed the landscape of their institutions.

Each author is a faculty or administrator currently at one of the nation's Historically Black Colleges and Universities (HBCUs). Their efforts to transform their campuses to advance diversity and inclusion in STEM, especially for women of color, are often grounded in an inner spirit - or "soul" - that permeates much of the HBCU culture that reflects the belief that those who have "arrived" have done so through "standing on the shoulders" of others. The "others" are elders (and s/heroes) who sacrificed much or paid great dues for the current generation to advance. The unspoken expectation is that members of the current generation must do likewise for the next generation. In short, a "calling" to Lead!

Finally, the chapters clearly reveal the notion that college and university leaders may come from numerous perches, i.e., those with formal leadership titles like Dean, Chair, etc., but also from highly respected faculty and staff members. Strong departments, institutions, and, indeed, disciplines are typically characterized by strong leaders – that is, intellectual icons, visionaries, effective communicators, and astute administrators. Again, no matter the source, for true institutional impact *Leaders Matter!*

INTRODUCTION

We Need You at the Table: Being
Vulnerable and Making the Sacrifice

Stephanie Luster-Teasley, PhD

The first time I applied for full professor, my promotion was denied. I had applied early despite knowing that historically anyone that applied early in my College was typically denied. Part of me was optimistic that my years of hard work would overcome the traditional rejection and that my successful performance post-promotion to associate professor would lead to favorable consideration for early promotion. The realist part of part of me, however, knew it would probably be a rejection and I wanted to have the feedback from the review to know where the holes were in my dossier. Risky, yes, because it opened me up for scrutiny and the ultimate career vulnerability.

Well, the fairy tale didn't happen and I received the rejection letter. The committee was split with half applauding my teaching, service, research, mentoring, grants, publications and patents. The other half felt I needed more time with the recommendation to secure more disciplinary grants and to write more disciplinary publications. As an assistant professor working towards associate professor, I was dedicated to being a solid teacher, writing grants, and my water remediation research. I felt my potential impact as a role model was important because I was a young female faculty member with small children. I wanted to be successful because female faculty are underrepresented in STEM. I wanted to be a role model for my female students to show them that women with young families could compete with her male counterparts. I wanted to show my male students that women were solid engineers. I wanted to prove to my male faculty colleagues that a woman could achieve promotion and deserved equal treatment and review for promotion.

Once I became an Associate Professor, I was happy and felt secure. I continued my research, teaching and department service. I added to my passions pursuing outreach for middle school girls in STEM, training to increase the number of students pursuing graduate school, professional development for women faculty through our NSF ADVANCE Grant, and raising my elementary school and teenage sons. I was comfortable as an Associate Professor and doing the things for which I felt I was making a difference in the field and my family.

In 2014, I was part of a team that received a National Science Foundation ADVANCE grant to offer initiatives to help increase the number of women in academia progressing through the ranks. As part of our work, we studied the number of female and male faculty at the different academic levels. Our research determined that male faculty were evenly divided where 1/3 were at assistant, 1/3 were at associate and 1/3 were at full professor levels. Women faculty, on the other hand, were heavily concentrated by rank in the assistant and associate levels. In fact, less than 10% of our STEM female faculty were at the full professor rank. Our female faculty were in leadership roles as Directors and Chairs, but stuck at the associate level. Once the mandate was established for all chairs and upper level administrators to be at the full professor rank, this meant many of our women faculty would have limited opportunities to be considered for administrative roles.

The new requirement to be a Full Professor to be appointed for higher leadership roles at our university, hence, shifted the paradigm for many female faculty at my university. This trend that required Full Professorship was not new and is often part of the criteria at many universities. I realized that the true way to have impact in academia as a woman in STEM was to be at the leadership table. Not just as an Associate Professor, but the ability to have the title and the recognition befitting faculty who have reached full professorial level made a difference.

When I received my denial for promotion to full, I took the Retention, Tenure, and Promotion (RTP) committee's recommendation seriously and for two years focused on a plan to enhance my dossier. I had to step back from my love for outreach, training, and teaching. I often wondered if the sacrifice would be worth the reward if I were to be promoted. I debated if stepping back from my passions was the right thing to do for me and if the impact I would have as a full professor really mattered. After two years, I re-applied and was successfully promoted. Along my journey, I was also appointed to the Chairperson position for my department. Since reaching full professor and Chair, I have discovered that Full professorship really matters. Here is how I see we have more impact:

1. New Perspectives: The impact that a woman brings by being at the table for leadership decisions brings new perspectives to primarily male dominated decisions. Our ability to think holistically, collegially, and cooperatively helps when leading groups of faculty and building support.

2. Navigation: The recognition of promotion to the ranks affords one with the knowledge of how to navigate academia and the ability to help other faculty as they too move through aca-

demia. As women, often we are dedicated to our work but once we leave our "day jobs" we are often the primary caregivers for our families which include children, partners, sick or disabled family and aging family members. As tough as it may be, we have figured out how to "make it work" to balance career life and family life. WE can help men and women progress in their careers through our leadership.

3. Voice: Being able to sit at the table in an upper-level administrative position and "voice" your ideas, opinions, strategies, and decisions is probably the most impactful of all. When I was debating about applying for chair, one of my mentors told me, "the person who sits at the table in leadership helps shape the future."

So, my advice is, if you need to reach Full Professorship to be a Chair, Dean, Vice Chancellor, Vice President, Provost or President, making the sacrifice is worth it. It is worth taking the leap to achieve your ultimate leadership or professional goal. *Hoping* that by virtue of your talent and hard work that you will ultimately reach full professorship and higher administration is not guaranteed. Another one of my mentors likes to say, "Hope is not a strategy". She is absolutely correct. Hope is NOT a strategy. You must be open to your successes, as well as, areas where you need to grow to be promoted. You may need to look deep into the vulnerable areas of your portfolio and identify strategies for how to meet the requirements at your university, other universities and in your discipline. Through all of the bumps and bruises, be mindful of the impact you will have once you are a Chair, Dean or the Chancellor. Be mindful of your passions and pursue them but also know how to listen to the rules for how you will be evaluated, reviewed and promotion through the ranks. Women are needed to impact change to improve the rules, to make them better, more equitable, and dismantle biases that persist in academia. More and more women are obtaining STEM degrees and PhDs and we need their voices to help implement changes to improve the academic environment. Female STEM faculty, we need you at the table!

PART I

THE PATH TO FULL PROFESSOR

CHAPTER 1

Finding My Way on the Road Less Travelled
Tamara Floyd Smith, Ph.D., P.E.

Establishing the Context of My Experience

I am an African American female who was eligible for a full Pell Grant when entering college. I came from a loving home of two parents who were married for 48 years – until death. The marriage produced four children who survived past infancy, one boy and three girls. My brother is the oldest and I am second. My brother fit the profile of an engineer because he was always tinkering and investigating bicycles and radios. I was an avid reader who happened to be very good at math. My middle school teacher told me that if you are good at math and science, you should become an engineer. At the time, I thought that she was wrong because I knew that I wasn't a tinkerer like my brother. However, I was a very respectful child so I just listened without disagreeing.

The same teacher recommended me for the Joseph Baldwin Academy (JBA) for Eminent Young Scholars at what was then Northeast Missouri State University in Kirksville, MO. I was accepted, and the principal of my school and the community raised money so that I could attend the summer after my 7th grade year. The experience changed my life. I learned that I had some disadvantages like the fact that I was a first generation college student, which translated to me needing to navigate college without parental guidance. However, I had some advantages like the ability to focus for hours. During the program, some of the participants would start to squirm, but I just sat there and was able to complete most of a semester long college math course in just three weeks. I returned to my home school ready for the next math course. Sadly, my school only offered pre-algebra so three of my classmates and I repeated the book that we had completed the previous year. I returned to JBA the summer after eighth grade with financial assistance from my extended family. That summer, I finished the book and was able to successfully pass the CLEP test for college algebra and trigonometry (if my memory serves me correctly).

As I entered high school, I was able to take math classes with grades above me and by my senior year, I sat in the library with a calculus book teaching myself because there was no one else in the school to take the class with me. I became stuck midway through the book and asked the math teacher for help. He was a brilliant man, but I think he forgot some of the details of calculus because he hadn't seen it since he was an undergraduate decades before. Consequently, I stalled in my progress, but after matriculating to college and enrolling in Calculus, I learned that I had taught myself all of Calculus I and became stuck early in what was Calculus II. In hindsight, I don't know why I became stuck because the concept wasn't that difficult. It was essentially calculating the area between two curves. I think the issue was that, in the process of teaching myself, I never really grasped what calculus was. I could complete the calculations, but I really needed someone to explain what it was and show me the applications. Another explanation is that the book that I was provided in high school was an edition from the 1960's. I probably would have fared better with the book that I used as an undergraduate which had more illustrations and real world applications.

By senior year, I was valedictorian and a National Achievement Scholar. I was receiving recruitment materials from all over the nation. I was flipping through materials from Auburn University when I saw that the list of engineering majors was longer than mechanical and electrical. They were probably in alphabetical order. When I reached "chemical engineering" on the list, I was convinced that I could follow my middle school teacher's advice and become an engineer.

I was admitted to and received scholarships to all of the schools to which I applied. If my memory serves me correctly, they were Auburn University, Georgia Tech, Tuskegee University and University of Alabama. I limited myself to schools with chemical engineering programs. My most lucrative scholarship was from the University of Alabama. I was planning to attend in the Fall. However, I needed something to do for the summer. I learned about the Freshman Accelerated Start Up Training for Retention in the Engineering Curricula (FASTREC) program at Tuskegee University (TU) and applied. I was accepted and attended. I enjoyed the summer bridge program so much that I decided to attend TU in the fall. I entered college with AP credit for English composition thanks to a wonderful English teacher in high school who is responsible for my score of 4/5. I attended TU and completed a B.S. in chemical engineering four years later in 1996. I had four full time job offers, and I had applied to two graduate schools – University of Michigan and MIT. I was admitted to both and received fellowships to both. Ultimately, I decided to attend MIT because I had a good experience there at a summer program after my junior year. I chose an excellent advisor and made life-long friends while in graduate school. I completed an M.S. in chemical engineering practice and Ph.D. in chemical engineering. Then, I accepted a position in industry and worked there for two years prior to joining the faculty at Tuskegee University.

Stage 1: Assistant to Associate Professor – Securing Provisions
A former TU president often quoted Cyrus the Great when offering leadership lessons. I hadn't read it in 2003, but my mindset was certainly consistent with the Larry Hedrick translation which states "You'll always be on better terms with your allies if you can secure your own provisions."

When I arrived at my institution from industry, it was with a significant cut in salary and no start-up package. However, I knew exactly what I was getting into and my lifestyle was not structured for my industrial salary. In fact, it hadn't changed significantly since being a graduate student receiving a $25K per year fellowship. I knew that I either needed to save money from my academic year salary or identify summer employment to survive for the summer. Fortunately, I was able to do both and for two years I was an Office of Naval Research (ONR) fellow conducting research at ONR. This opportunity gave me access to infrastructure to be able to publish and provide the foundation for grant writing. These opportunities provided summer support, and I worked after hours to write proposals for grant funding. Eventually, the work paid off and I had enough grant support to pay my own summer salary.

On a personal note, I met my husband at a Christmas party that mutual friends were giving in 2003. We were married in 2005. I was never a person who dreamed about a fairy tale wedding, but it was nice that I had saved money to live on from my academic year salary and earned a salary at ONR which provided provisions to pay for a wedding.

The next hurdle was to conduct the research. To my dismay, I found that there wasn't a TU administrator who was monitoring grant success and allocating laboratory space accordingly. I had grant funding but no space allocation for the equipment that I ordered. Prior to approaching administrators, I decided that I would determine the minimum amount of space that I needed to get started and negotiate relentlessly for it. I didn't have a plan B for what happened if the negotiations stalled. I have a memory of standing in the space that I planned to request and explaining that if I could have just that I could get started. It wasn't straightforward because the constituents were very territorial. However, in the end I was given the approximately 50 sq ft. to fit the microscope that I ordered and to prepare solutions and devices. I knew that I would need more space once I identified undergraduates and graduate student researchers because it was only enough space for one to two people at a time. I focused on the positive. My equipment was delivered, and we configured it. Shortly thereafter, another faculty member left and I moved into his space without explicitly requesting it. I laugh now because my strategy was to be a squatter. The timing was perfect because as my group was expanding other faculty members were leaving, and I just took over the space. In the end, I had all the space that I needed and it was never "officially" given to me. The downside of this approach is that years later I was asked to address some issues that previous researchers left behind. Once I explained the situation, it was resolved but I made a mental note that squatting vs. a clean start can lead to problems like what I experienced. After four years, I applied for promotion from Assistant to Associate Professor. My package was successful and my era of focusing on providing my own provisions, as Cyrus the Great suggested, was over. Provisions still needed to be provided, but I compare it to the point in one's personal life when the coffers are full enough such that nothing new could come in for a while, but all would still be well.

Stage 2: Associate to Tenure – Adding Value

I had read the Faculty Handbook multiple times. Sometimes I would chuckle because it was marked in different color highlighters and pens reminding me that I had visited the pages many times.

I knew that I could check all of the boxes for tenure. Checking boxes is important because it is difficult for supporters to fight for you when you don't meet minimum requirements. In addition to checking the boxes, I began to think about my legacy and how to add value to the institution. I asked myself "Isn't that what tenure is about?" It is a lifetime commitment to a person – much like marriage. When choosing to commit to someone, doesn't the reviewer need to have a vision of the value of that person to the organization?

"Wasn't it about the time you came on board
that I turned the company around?"

My promotion to Associate Professor came around the time that my first son was born. Interestingly, in spite of playing organized sports from middle school through high school and having professional physicals, I wasn't aware of a sickle cell trait or beta thalassemia until I was pregnant. I felt fine, but I did spiral momentarily. I remember telling my mother that I had a trait and informing her that it had to come from either my mother or my father. My mother vehemently proclaimed "It was your father." Well, further research revealed it was my mother. Perhaps, the most disturbing aspect is that my mother had five live births without knowing that she had a sickle cell trait. Apart from the discovery of two prior unknown disorders, my pregnancy was uneventful. The birth was also fairly uneventful. Motherhood was challenging because of the unpredictability of illnesses. My son had very frequent ear infections and it took us almost two years to discover that he had a milk protein allergy. It turns out that I have the same allergy so within two years of motherhood I was up to three previously undiscovered disorders.

While juggling motherhood, I tackled a problem that we were having with classroom allocations in my building. When I joined the faculty, I was told that the issue of classroom space was caused by a building being offline. When the building came online, the issue persisted. I pressed for an explanation, but in the end the solution offered was that the first person to the classroom gets it. I found that approach unacceptable so I created a spreadsheet of all the courses scheduled in the building. Very quickly, I discovered the problem – we had too many MWF classes from 9-11a and not enough TTH classes. It seems trivial, but it was a problem that I solved – at least temporarily. Once the problem was solved, I recall strongly opposing any suggestion to move a class to the MWF 9-11a time slot. I would show the spreadsheet from a few years back as the reason why we needed to be careful. My advice wasn't followed, but at least I knew what that problem was. It was my first lesson in administration and how unreasonable some highly educated people can be. The moral of the story is that, if only for one year, the problem of classroom allocations was solved and that was clear value that I added with my own initiative.

During this period of time, I may have peaked in my review activity both for funding agencies and journals. I felt it was important to add value not only to my institution, but also to my field. I developed my identity as a reviewer. One key core value was that every document deserved my full attention. Even if I didn't think an article should be published or a proposal should be funded, it was my responsibility to provide useful feedback to allow for continuous improvement. I felt this was an important part of my leadership development because "only those who serve the people deserve to rule the people" (Hedricks, 2006, pg. 247).

I became a licensed engineer as a faculty member and participated in an Order of the Engineer ceremony. I had the idea to start a link at my institution. I approached the Dean with my idea and he was supportive. However, he informed me that someone had the idea prior to me but that person didn't get it off the ground. I think it was a statement to suggest that it was hard in case I didn't succeed. I walked out of the meeting thinking, "Oh, it will get done on my watch." We visited a chapter in the state to see their ceremony and then we began the process to initiate our Link. Since that time, we have held the ceremony continuously and it has grown to be an important aspect of commencement for engineering students.

Ultimately, I received notification that I was granted tenure at my institution. What was most important to me is that if I hadn't been awarded tenure, I was confident that I would "fail forward" because my portfolio clearly illustrated my value.

Stage 3: Tenure to Full Professor – Sustainability
Entering this timeframe, I had tenure. However, I didn't want to be dead wood. I had seen other colleagues who weren't produc-

tive and my conscience wouldn't let me choose that path. I knew that I wanted to be promoted to full professor, but I was thinking beyond that point to retirement.

My context in higher education was that I was working at a private, HBCU. In addition to Title III funding, there are other funds that have been specifically dedicated to minority serving institutions or primarily undergraduate institutions. Many of the opportunities were competitive, but the field of competition was obviously limited to institutions that met the criteria. Early in my career, I had been pursued for opportunities because I was the person that PIs wanted to work with at an HBCU. Going forward, I wanted to be known as the person that other PIs wanted to work with independent of my institutional context. Moreover, earlier in my career, I found myself pursing research opportunities that ultimately left me diffuse in my research. My goals for the purposes of sustainability was to focus. My concern was that it would appear to my administration that I was "slowing down." My administration seemed to not mind if, as PIs, our research was diffuse. But I knew that it was counterproductive to be being at the top of the field and/or winning major awards.

During this period, I made an effort to integrate teaching and research. I shed one course that didn't align and began teaching one that aligned best. In this way, I could use research articles and research lab demonstrations to enhance the classroom experience.

I also worked on an NSF-funded project that changed my approach to undergraduate education. It was a collaborative effort with other institutions and it was my first formal introduction to active learning methods. Another feature of the project is that we studied the relationship between belonging and engagement. It was my first consideration of how important affective factors are for student performance. I transformed the introductory course that I was teaching to include a professional engagement component to the grade which included reflection papers, engagement with professional societies, career fair attendance etc.

Additionally, at this point, I was expecting my second child. In order to better align my career with motherhood, I increased my focus on K12 outreach. Research on what children do was part of motherhood so it made perfect sense that I would integrate it with my academic research because I was already immersed in the literature and practice. My K12 outreach research centered on the design of activities for K12 students that led to an increase in knowledge of and interest in STEM. I found that, much like my own children, most children enjoy hands-on activities. They also like engaging videos. They like to connect to their favorite shows. As an example, I use the movie "Up" to teach buoyancy. Later I discovered, that the approaches that I used in K12 were also useful for my undergraduates.

Managing one child was difficult but managing two children felt like more than a factor of two increase. Whereas I previously was able to work during naps, the oldest wasn't napping anymore so that strategy wasn't applicable with the second child. My youngest was lactose intolerant. That was discovered quickly, but he also had an intestinal problem that would flare up occasionally. My package for promotion was submitted as I was leaving for maternity leave. I felt that it was a strong package, and, indeed, I was promoted to Full Professor.

My package for promotion to full professor highlighted ten peer reviewed journal publications in the last five years while maintaining a full teaching load (3 courses per semester without assistance from teaching assistants), fourteen abstracts and/or conference proceeding publications, eight presentations of scholarly work, preparation of a laboratory guide for a course, leadership in professional organizations as session chair or co-chair at national meetings and more than $2M of external funding as institutional principal investigator. Within three years of promotion, I had served as major professor for 2 Ph.D. degrees, 3 M.S. degrees and supervised more than 30 undergraduates in undergraduate research. Although mentorship wasn't a category to qualify for promotion, it was my proudest accomplishment.

Stage 4: Beyond Full Professor 2012-2015 - Stackable Credentials

By the time I was promoted to Full Professor, I began to experience some frustration. I had done the work and earned a seat a table, but I felt that I wasn't being heard. Instinctively, I thought that becoming an administrator would solve the problem. However, no position was available. Was I to remain powerless for decades until a position opened? And when it did, who is to say that

I would have been chosen? Around the time that these thoughts were swirling, I attended a professional conference with a session on "influencing without authority." It was my first introduction to the various power categories outlined by French & Raven (2006).

Going forward, my goal would be to position myself to influence without legitimate authority. I was already a full professor and, therefore, a subject matter expert. My next step was to become an ABET evaluator so that I would have informational power as it relates to accreditation and simultaneously be able to engage my core value of assisting with continuous improvement in my reviewer context. Lastly, I decided to pursue an academic leadership credential. Around the time that I made the decision, I learned of the NSF-funded Opportunities for UnderRepresented Scholars (OURS) program. I took advantage of the opportunity and learned more about power, authentic leadership, leadership styles, achieving flow and many other leadership principles. As part of the program, we received coaching, and we were required to complete an action learning project at our home institutions. Upon completion of the program, I felt ready for leadership. My preparation intersected an opportunity leading to success and the second phase of my academic career – administration.

References

French, J. R., Jr. & Raven, B. (2006). The Bases of Social Power. In J.L. Pierce and J. W. Newstrom (Eds.), Leaders and the Leadership Process (4th ed., pp. 146-152). New York, NY: McGraw Hill.

Hedrick, Larry. (2006). *Xenophon's Cyrus the Great: The Arts of Leadership and War*. New York: Truman Talley Books.

Maxwell, John C. (2000). *Failing Forward: Turning Mistakes Into Stepping Stones for Success*. Nashville, TN: Thomas Nelson, Inc.

CHAPTER 2

What Does Not Kill You Will Make You Stronger

Nicole Smith, PhD*

I had just endured the toughest two years of my personal life when I started a master's degree program in STEM. To make matters worse, no one in my department had ever seen an African-American female before, especially one who was in pursuit of a graduate degree in STEM. I am sure the only black women they had ever seen were black women who cleaned their houses or watched their children. In the minds of many faculty members, they did not think that I was capable of doing the work, and they wanted to make sure that I failed.

None of the members in the department were women and none of them were people of color. In their minds, my STEM discipline belonged to them, white men. When I say *them,* I am not limiting the sabotage to faculty members; I am also talking about the students who were also biased. One way that the students worked against me is in their refusal to include me in group projects. In fact, all of the students avoided working with me. In their minds, I had nothing to contribute to the conversation or to their understanding of the field. To make matters worse, I also had a strange relationship with the Teaching Assistants (TAs). Because the school that I attended was a research school, faculty as well as TAs taught the courses and graded all of the papers. Their presence in the courses were not consistent like the faculty in the department; there would be a different TA in every class. Teaching classes and grading papers for the master's program is how the TAs made money to pay for school; on the other hand, word got out that my tuition and expenses were being paid-in-full. I was on a full ride. The university had extended to me a full scholarship that paid for tuition, books, fees, room/board and a hearty stipend. My only job was to attend school and graduate; therefore, the same TAs that taught me in some classes were also the TAs who were in my classes as fellow students. They resented the fact that I did not have to work to pay for school. They also resented the fact that I had the nerve to be in the same class as them, working on the same degree.

As a result of their resentment, I was graded unfairly by these TAs compared to the other students. Unfortunately, I did not feel comfortable enough with anyone in the department to discuss my concerns. One time, I had shared a concern I had about the department with a faculty member whom I thought I could trust, and I was told, "Don't come around here throwing the race card. You will have to work like everyone else." I cannot begin to explain the depression, the feelings of defeat, and the embarrassment that I felt on a constant basis. I learned that they do not hear or accept excuses of any kind. They certainly did not want to hear about the racism or sexism that operated in their department. In addition, I often felt that they were evaluating my character rather than the merits of my academic performance. Substantive comments were never written on my paper; instead, micro-aggressive notes were often scribbled on them. For example, one time instead of providing academic feedback, one instructor wrote "Great Stick-it-to-ativeness." Is that even a word?

On another occasion, I had scored a perfect grade on a homework assignment and was accused of cheating. The TA told the professor that I must have copied someone else's work, but he could not prove it. After reading the accusation, I called the TA on the telephone in front of the professor with my actual homework in my hand. The TA could tell me verbatim what my answers were and how I could not have gotten them correct without cheating. There were about thirty-four other students in the class. How did he remember my paper in such detail? I asked if there were any others that had received a perfect score and he said "of course." However, why was I the only one being accused of cheating? I drove back home that weekend and told my parents that I was never going back to that school ever again. My parents agreed that there had to have been some major importance to the degree. They surmised that it must have been a "high dollar" field and that I was to do the best I could and continue. So my parents said a group prayer, drove me back to school and said, "You can do this." And I did. I dug deeper in my inner self, prayed, had daily discussions with my support group and worked harder to continue to make more perfect score assignments. I wanted them to know that this was not a fluke and that I was smart. I went to the library on campus every day and studied every book that had anything to do with what I was learning. I knew the library so well, I could have gotten a job as a librarian. Working so hard to make every-one else think that I was smart allowed me to start to have some confidence in myself and to understand that I am really smart. So, when I completed the Master's degree, I couldn't believe that I was to continue being abused in similar ways by pursuing a doc-toral degree in a larger metropolitan city, but I was. Only this time, the abuse came from someone who I thought would be my advocate.

I was told that obtaining a doctoral degree would be better for my career and that there was a huge need for women of color in STEM. As a result, the school would find a company to sponsor my tuition, books, room and board and double my stipend amount that I received while earning my master's degree. They held up their end of the bargain, so I said okay. With two children and a husband in tow, I moved forward.

It was in my doctoral program that I met the first white female with a terminal degree in my STEM discipline, and she meant business. She was my dissertation advisor, and I wrongfully thought that we were supposed to be on the same team. We met often and we met hard. She drilled me, pledged me, and insulted me in ways that Miranda Priestly, played by Meryl Streep, in the movie, *The Devil wears Prada* did to the characters Andy and Emily. The comments were so direct and harsh towards me. Because she often commented about how fresh and relaxed I looked, I began to believe that she begrudged the pride that I took about my appearance. So I decided that meeting with her in the future that I should not look so "put together" and relaxed." I would intentionally put a run in my pantyhose and would wash my face to remove my makeup before I went to see her. I felt that if she thought I was not suffering she would make sure that I did.

Part of her pledging process was to have me use my skills in computer science outside of academia. She would often demand that I work pro bono for her family and friends. For instance, I was often tasked to work for her husband and church people in her community. I was often asked to meet her at her home on numerous occasions. I met her children and parents and was told not to say too much. To make matters worse, I had to endure name calling, and racists questions that she had about African Americans that had absolutely nothing to do with computer science: "Why are there no African American males at home?" and "Why would African American children kill each other over basketball shoes?" I felt as if I had to answer for the entire race instead of focus on my scientific abilities. I have several memories of these conversations that still haunt me to this day. Oddly, when I took a step back, I realize that I learned so much during this stage of my life. I learned that patience, perseverance, strategy, humility and of course prayer always work no matter what.

I realized that she had no idea that I was on a full academic scholarship, and she wondered how I could afford the cost of the tuition. One of her major projects for the university was to increase the number of minorities in STEM; however, the only thing that she really knew about African-American women were the derogatory stereotypes that she saw on television, where black women were always impoverished and less achieving. There were two other African-American females in the pipeline at the university to earn doctoral degrees in my STEM discipline and none of us matched the negative views of minority women that she had in her mind. Although the three of us would talk, we never discussed our treatment in the department. We kept that to ourselves. I have often asked myself why didn't we talk. Is it because we are supposed to feel inferior, or were we too proud to say that we are struggling? Maybe we were just so busy juggling everything in our lives -- family, full-time jobs and school assignments. Maybe we had no choice but to go through the program and just do it. Looking back, I wish we would have talked about our struggles in the program. A major part of success is learning how to communicate with one another and gain support. Together we are so much smarter.

On another occasion, I had just found out that I was pregnant with my third child, and I told my advisor that I was pregnant. Her response was, "I think that you should have it." My all-time favorite mean- spirited comment from her was at the end of my program right before the defense of my dissertation. She told me three things would happen at the end of the defense: The committee would reject the entire defense, and I would not be allowed to start over; they would reject the defense with major modifications; or they would tell me to go home because what I had produced was not dissertation material. None of her comments were positive, and I knew that I had worked very hard on the dissertation document and the results. Just to let you know the final decision of the defense--the entire committee signed off on it, and there were absolutely no changes that needed to be made. I was the second African-American female to earn a doctoral degree in my STEM field at that University.

So here I am to date, one of the first pioneering women of color with a doctoral degree in my STEM discipline, and I am working for a Historically Black University. Ironically, almost every faculty of seventeen members in the department were non-African American and male. I thought working at a historically black college would give me the feelings of being home. In my mind, this HBCU would represent a place where I belonged where I no longer had to deal with racism or sexism. After all, I received my bachelor's degree from a Historically Black University. I just knew that I would find a strong mentor that understood my pain and struggles. This mentor would embrace me and show me the path to success and feeling more self-confident. Little did I know, that the obstacles that I had previously faced were mild compared to the struggles that I would have to endure as a faculty member in my department on an HBCU campus. After all, I was the only African American in the Department with a terminal degree in the field itself. For the next 18 years, I was going for a ride similar to being on a wild horse.

It was on this campus that I met and befriended an African American female colleague. She was not a "Mentor" but a "Tormentor". She never wanted to move the department forward; instead, her mission was to stop all progress. The Tormentor was a tenured-full professor at this HBCU. She was 10-years-older than me. We had gotten off to a pretty good start as long as I was her pet. I had always done what she said and how she told me to do it. As the years went by, things got rocky between us when I started to grow into my strengths in hiring, chairing committees on campus, getting known across campus for working hard and getting things done. I had even served as chair of the College Curriculum Committee for 7 years; presided as Chair of the General Education Committee and managed to have complete buy-in for the general education revamp during the first seven months of my service. Somehow, The Tormentor began to view me differently. In fact in The Tormentor's mind, I went from being her pet to becoming a threat to her in eight years.

Then the unthinkable happened. She began to circulate ugly lies about me on campus. Because The Tormentor had social influence, her voice mattered. Everyone on campus believed her mean and hurtful remarks that my degree did not mean anything, and that I did not know anything, nor did I do any work. One other thing that The Tormentor had to her advantage was her knowledge about the faculty handbook. In fact, she knew all of the policies and procedures like the names of the months of the year because she was one of the original authors. Her knowledge of policies allowed her to practically run the campus as other faculty were not as abreast as she. In fact, everyone on campus assumed that when she spoke about campus policy, it must be campus law. She used this authority to block everything that was innovative or could improve the university's visibility.

Despite my achievements on campus, my tenure was rejected once and was overturned by the University Committee for Tenure and Promotion. Sadly, my promotions were always rejected. I applied for full professorship four times. Each time I was rejected, but the very last time was cruel and a very lowly attempt to damage my character despite my achievements.

After losing accreditation from a non-governmental organizations that accredits post-secondary education programs in applied science, computing, engineering, and engineering technology, I was nominated to serve as chair of the department. One of my first tasks was to have our departmental accreditation reinstated. None of the members of the department seemed to care enough about our dire state to do the work to have our credentials renewed; instead, they decided to sit it out and watch the department die a slow death, which would have resulted in me being viewed as a failed chair, which is exactly what they wanted. Without accreditation, enrollment would reduce as well as the possibilities of grant awards from federal agencies. None of this mattered to the faculty. They decided that they cared more about winning a personal vendetta against me instead of the well-being of our students.

By 2012, the department had grown to consist of three additional African-American women in my discipline, which was unheard of across the United States. It was these three women who volunteered to help move the department forward. We worked every day until eleven o'clock p.m. for one month to write the department's plan to be reinstated. As a team, we worked like lionesses on the hunt. Our hard work was not in vain, in exactly thirty-one days of constant hard work, we submitted the final report. When the accreditation team arrived on campus and learned about how we turned things around, we were told that our accreditation would be reinstated without conditions or warnings. This was the first time in the department's history that we had a clean accreditation report from the accreditation team. This is when the university started to notice that the four African-American women from my department were workers and finishers. The word on campus was that "The African American Women in that department" were smart. The Tormentor did not like this too much, but regardless of her thoughts, the other three African-American women, and I published a peer-reviewed paper that earned a peer-reviewed score of 98% about how to obtain accreditation so that we could help other universities.

Another major accomplishment for me was a grant that I collaborated with an industry leader wrote. I worked with an industry leader to assist the university in being the lead of a multi-million dollar grant. To get the grant, I was asked by The Chief Operating Officer of the organization that could award the grant to do a presentation on cybersecurity in front of the Board of Directors for the University Research & Development Foundation (URDF) in Washington, D.C. The presentation was so impressive that the grantor visited the campus president. Following the grantor's visit was a presentation among competing universities/colleges to select the lead of the grant. The Tormentor was not invited to the presentation but she told one of our male colleagues how to act to make sure that the university did get the lead. That colleague performed so much so that he had memory loss and forgot we were colleagues. He voted for a competing intuition to be the lead. I could not move, get up or turn around to see his face. I had a forty-minute hot flash in my seat! Due to The Tormentor's mission to degrade, humiliate, embarrass and show of displeasure of me in front of fifty people from other institutions, the grantor as well as industry representatives at that presentation, the university was not granted the lead but was awarded $1.2 million.

Another notable accomplishment were the connections that were made for our department to over 20 industry and government partnerships such as Northrop Grumman, Lockheed Martin, National Security Agency (NSA), National Aeronautics and Space Administration (NASA), Goddard, Department of Homeland Security Honeywell, and IBM to name a few. These relationships were vital to securing an additional $1.5 million in grant funding plus provided countless internship opportunities for our students. On October 2014, I applied for full professor. Somehow, The Tormentor did it again. She did the unthinkable, especially from someone who should have been a sister. She turned the entire department of 18 faculty members against me and accused me as well as the other three African-American women of scholarly misconduct. I immediately had to figure out how to protect the other three women because none of them had tenure or a voice in the department.

The first step I took was to appeal my denial of the promotion. I won the appeal, but the president of the university did not agree with the appeals committee; therefore, I was not granted the promotion. The next thing that we did was to file a grievance on campus. To do this we worked hard to look at multiple interpretations of the faculty handbook and presented our case. We worked so hard on the grievance that the university's counsel thought it was prepared by a lawyer. That's when the university called in an additional lawyer. After the grievance committee heard our case, they found several wrongdoings by The Tormentor and made some suggestions about separating the two programs in the department into two separate departments. They also recommended that I get the promotion for full professor. Of course the president of the campus ruled against the grievance committee and denied any wrong doings on behalf of the university. I had no choice but to file a Federal Employee Equal Opportunity Commission (EEOC) complaint.

During this process the three African-American women and I, agreed to stop marching to everyone else's orders in the department and to focus on teaching the students and doing our work like we always had done instead of partnering on grants with the department, and serving on outside committees. Instead, we dedicated our energies to locating grants that funded our interests, publishing, attending conferences, and presenting our research. It was soon noticed across the campus that the department was dysfunctional and no work was getting done by the other 18 faculty members who were our adversaries. Our department that once had a reputation for being an elitist department on campus was no longer viewed as the golden one. The department was getting a bad reputation and others on campus no longer saw the faculty members in the department as having strong minds but as non-workers. The very things that The Tormentor accused me of was what the campus started to see her and in the department among the other faculty members. In the end, I finally received my promotion and all of us started to receive the respect that we deserved.

Looking back, I was made to feel that I did not belong in any academic settings. The faculty in both my master's and doctoral degree programs refused to take my scholarly abilities seriously. They did this by scribbling non-substantive remarks on my papers, accusing me of cheating on homework assignments, and making light of the sexism and racism that existed in their departments. During my doctoral program, I was required to help family and friends of my dissertation chair in ways that were not helpful toward my studies. Furthermore, I also had to endure name calling and other comments in an attempt to discourage me. As a college educator at an HBCU campus, a powerful woman on campus made me her personal enemy and tried her best to turn the university against me. Everything that I tried to do, she tried to block.

In spite of it all, I have learned to move forward past the adversity through the help of support groups, prayer, and team-work. I would encourage you to commit to a team you can trust and work together. If you are not able to build a team where you are, build a team elsewhere within your surrounding area. In addition, continue to publish, attend conferences and work on different committees in order to build social capital. Always be honest, forthright, and work with integrity. Integrity is BIG. You must always be noted as an honest person to maintain trust. Also, believe in yourself, and be patient. You are not alone, you are smart enough, and you do belong. Tormentors will always be a big part of your pathway to success. How do you plan to deal with them? I am the first to tell you that you must have a plan. The first step of your plan is to work around them and move forward. Do not let them pull you in their direction because it will not lead to your success but your failure and short comings. In the end, I am glad that I had to fight. I find that I am not bitter or angry. Each hurdle that I accomplished lead me closer to another success. Because what I have learned through it all is that what did not kill me made me stronger.

*Pseudonym

CHAPTER 3

I belong here!
Michelle Olivia Fletcher Claville, PhD

I am Michelle Olivia Fletcher Claville, Ph.D. I am a wife of one, a mother of two, a Professor of Chemistry, an Assistant Dean for a School of Science, a scientist, a researcher, and so much more. I have a story to tell - one that I did not realize was worth of telling, until now. Like many stories, it is a story of intrigue, romance, adventure and conflict. It is a story of disappointment and resilience, of heartbreak and triumph, of loneliness and friendship, of fear, faith and favor. This story is about accepting my place in the academy, and tells about my path to attaining the coveted rank of *Full Professor.*

I did not always know that I was going to be a professor of chemistry. In fact, as a little girl growing up in Jamaica, West Indies, I did not understand that there were other types of doctors beside medical doctors. In fact, I thought that my aptitude for science and love for humanity must have meant that I was destined to practice medicine. After all, I had not been exposed to diversity of intellectual professions that some of international neighbors enjoyed. Furthermore, I had watched just enough episodes of *Marcus Welby, MD, Trapper John, MD,* and *Julie Farr, MD* to convince myself that I was going to grow up to be Michelle Fletcher, M.D.

After I completed high school, I immigrated to the United States. I then performed my due diligence by enrolling in college, choosing the appropriate science major (in my case, Chemistry), engaging in the necessary extra-curricular activities, and guarding that ever important grade point average (GPA). I was so protective of my GPA that I even changed my major to English during the last 18 months of college. After all, I had already completed my pre-requisite courses for entry into medical school. And so, I used my last year to pursue my other love, the literary arts, pass the medical school admissions test, and engage in the appropriate extra-curricular activities. I did everything necessary to get accepted into medical school and succeeded in the same. In 1990, I joined a class of about 130 other students as a first year medical student at the University of Miami's (UM) Medical School. I had made my family proud, while confounding others who thought that I should not succeed in my efforts.

Not surprisingly, my classmates and I were all excited and optimistic; but some of us were also uncertain. At twenty-one years old, I finally had to address nagging thoughts that questioned my fit for a profession of medicine. You see, after migrating to the US, for the first time in my life, I had to engage with people who thought that I was aspiring for a position that was not meant for me. I recall one professor asking me why I was doing all of this, "just to go have some babies" and drop out. I also recall the voice of one family member who encouraged me to be a nurse or "go work with computers," or something desk-oriented. If that wasn't enough, I also had to deal with my own thoughts that longed to discover and utilize other talents, like English and the Arts. I had come from a long line of educators and exhibited the same traits. Was I meant to be a medical doctor, or not?

My thoughts argued with each other for months, some claiming that I had to stay faithful to "the dream of being the first Fletcher MD", while others begged me to investigate ME.

Should I stay or walk away? Should I make everyone else happy, or should I be certain that I was truly happy? Was I giving in to the naysayers, or was this an honest inquiry? Could I walk away from a scholarship to one of the best medical schools in the country? Could I face my family? What would my friends, fans and foes say if I walked away? The internal noise was so loud that I had address it. After praying, I received the necessary peace and strength to retreat for a year in order to determine my future in medicine.

It was difficult dealing with the constant questions and critiques from loved ones and skeptics who chose to believe that I wasn't smart enough to succeed in medical school. Please understand that I kept up a *proper* public face, but privately wept because of the unresolved uncertainty within me. I attended classes to keep my mind fresh, just in case I should return to UM, but eventually, yielded to the realization that my path was not in medicine and elected not to return to medical school. I was plagued by my own thoughts that declared failure, especially in the face of others who begrudged my right to that place of accomplishment. My heart was full of sorrow and begged to know what my path was. The absence of an answer worried me and pushed me to embrace the negativity of my skeptics. I became quiet and resolved to get a job *somewhere* after earning my second Bachelor's degree in Chemistry.

Even though I thought that I was working in apparent isolation, I soon recognized that some of my professors had been observing me, and recognized talent in me that they wished nurture. One encourage me to participate in a summer Research Experience for Undergraduate program which eventually led to an invitation to conduct research in the lab of a prominent researcher. That invitation led to another invitation to apply for graduate school in chemistry at the University of Florida, and to continue research in physical organic chemistry.

Nevertheless, after accepting an invitation, I remained in a mental space where I doubted my abilities. My lack of confidence showed in my classwork and invited unfair assessments of me. I was so forlorn, that I unwittingly permitted blatant proclivities against me UNTIL, that moment – that event- which forced me to declare, "NO MORE!" I had to emerge from that negative space in order to properly recognize and respond to discriminatory acts to which me and others like had been subject.

Now, by no means am I claiming that I instantly transformed into a Betty Shabazz or an Angela Davis. Instead, I am recognizing that I had to *WAKE UP* from the dazed state*!* While wallowing in past uncertainties, I had failed to realize that I was on the path meant for me. Moreover, I was allowing others to sabotage my progress as I docilely accepted their injustices. I had to *WAKE UP* and recognize who I was and to *Whom* I belonged. And so, I woke up.

I finally embraced the fact that I belonged in the field of chemistry, and I had every right to earn the doctorate. I was smart enough. I deserved the support and attention that others received. I deserved the opportunity to help others excel in chemistry. I had to act differently, and so I began to change. I learned new ways to study. I exercised my rights to ask questions, in and outside of class. The more I learned, the more I began recognizing the fallibility in those who were supposedly more favored than me. I began challenging unfair acts while acknowledging my weaknesses and working to correct my own deficiencies.

I attribute my successful completion of graduate school to

many. I benefited from the support of my predecessors (i.e. black females who overcame challenges to earn their doctorate degree in chemistry), friends, family members, church family, professors, post-docs, visiting scientists, NOBCChE, and everyone else who invested in me and supported my awakening. Their prayers, faith, patience, and encouragement helped usher me into a self-confident state that propelled me to the PhD degree. I also benefitted from those who were either micro-aggressors, unfair, or hindrances. They offended me just long enough for me to fight back. They did just enough for me to work harder and think smarter. They forced my resilience and awakened the realization that value did not lie in their perceptions and assessments.

My personal growth was accompanied by the realization that I was meant to be an educator. So, after four years in industry, I convinced a college dean in southern Louisiana to take a chance on hiring me as an Assistant Professor with a temporary/annual appointment. I was determined to be the best professor of organic chemistry they had. Furthermore, I had a mission to prepare as many students of color as I could for excellence in professional and graduate schools. By the next year, I convinced him to advocate for my transition to a probationary tenure-track position. After all, I needed that designation in order to apply for the National Science Foundation's Faculty Early Career Development (CAREER) award.

I had to learn how to juggle family and career very quickly. My second semester as an Assistant Professor began with my pregnancy with our first child. By the time our son was born – early by the way – I had written my first small grant, co-authored my first instrumentation proposal, and became the proposal editor for the university's Office of Sponsored Programs. I was determined to show naysayers that a black female professor at a historically black college/university (HBCU) was as competent as successful professors at predominantly white institution.

My fifth year as an academician was rewarded with the coveted CAREER award, tenure, promotion to Associate Professor and appointment as Department head. Moreover, I was the wife of a newly-graduated attorney, the mother of two boys, and a member of the ministerial team at my church. I was tired ALL the time, but I was content because I was fulfilling my purpose.

Any discontent that I had resulted from the realization that I had not escaped the nuances of politics, micro- (and macro-) aggressions and other types of injustices. I dealt with the disappointment of knowing that others violently begrudged my mission and the corresponding achievements. The weight was intensified because I was determined to excel as a wife and mother.

From time to time, I was reminded that I was not alone. I had (and still have) a husband that was (and still is) very supportive of me. He and other family members bragged on me when I did not even recognize that I was worthy of the accolades. I had colleagues and students who created an environment that nurtured my family. They provided a safe place that made me want to work without ever having to worry about the safety or neglect of my loved ones. I had advocates who trusted me to advance my department, and invested in my plans to update its research infrastructure. With their help, I was responsible for the purchase of multiple scientific instruments including a peptide synthesizer, an electron paramagnetic spectrometer, a mass spectrometer, an atomic absorption spectrometer, and so much more.

Eventually, another institution recruited me to become their assistant dean of science, albeit without tenure. After a great deal of counsel, consideration, and encouragement from my family, I accepted the offer with the intent of earning tenure again. I quickly accepted the subsequent charge to win another coveted award from the National Science Foundation (NSF) in the amount of three million dollars. With those funds, I could continue to change the world by preparing more students from underrepresented groups to excel in STEM fields, and pioneer a new nanoscience program at the institution. Meanwhile, I had to re-earn tenure.

With the support of my NSF program director, I hired a post-doctoral researcher who became instrumental in sustaining my laboratory research. Nevertheless, I remained tired as I still had to teach, serve in my administrative role, manage my $3M project, and maintain my research. Not only did I have a heavy load, but I still faced political nuances, and unfriendly competition. There were many who did not care if I received tenure, just as long as I did not reach the ranks of Full Professor. Those were the ones who did what they could to hinder that promotion.

Thankfully, my supporters outweighed my challengers. Without realizing it, I had gained allies who cheered me on, prayed for me, and provided additional opportunities for me to succeed. Before long, I had everything in place to successfully earn the rank of Professor, and I did.

In order to summarize my journey and encourage someone else, let me say the following. Be true to yourself. Never give up. Discover your true worth and recognize that is not necessarily the same as that which others perceive. Be kind to yourself. Establish your ethical boundaries and maintain them. Identify your true supporters. Never despise help from unconventional places. Create the environment that you need to truly succeed. Empower others to truly succeed. Be wary of shortcuts. Don't worry about the pace of *your* race; just be certain to finish it. If this is where you belong, then BELONG.

CHAPTER 4

Making an Impact on Alcorn State University: My Journey to Full Professorship

Sandra L. Barnes, PhD

Unto whomsoever much is given, of him shall be much required.

Luke 12:48

Preparation and Proper mentorship

In order to be successful at anything in life, one must make necessary preparations. I have not been the smartest person nor have I been the most well off person in life, but I do believe that my ability to prepare has been a key factor in reaching the full professorship. I knew that being at a Minority Serving Institution meant that I needed to excel in the areas of Teaching, Research, and Service. I believe a large part of my preparation came through advice and opportunities provided by mentors and associates who helped me to get off to a good start in my academic career at Alcorn. I am very grateful that I had mentors at that time who helped me understand some of the things that I needed to be doing.

One of those mentors was my undergraduate advisor, the late Dr. Thomas Bolden, who was a full professor of Biochemistry at Alcorn. He actually encouraged me to apply for the Biotechnology Research Assistant Professor position in the Biotechnology Center at Alcorn, my first position at Alcorn. First, he helped prepare me for the position by giving me pointers on who would make up the audience. He told me that I had to give a stellar presentation because there were those who did not believe that a young black woman, I was only thirty-one at the time, had anything to contribute to a biotechnology program. With his continued support and preparation, I was selected for the position.

After getting the position, he and the Chair of the Chemistry Department at the time, Dr. Troy Stewart, made sure that I started getting teaching experience right away by insisting that I teach biochemistry. Although I was very hesitant an unsure, they both insisted that I do it. This was a major step forward because if I had not begun to teach at that time, I would have been behind in regards to promotion and tenure in the area of teaching since my position was primarily a research position. Dr. Bolden also insisted that I join the graduate council by applying for graduate faculty status. At the time, I had no clue what this would do for me or the students, but he was a trusted mentor who had never led me down the wrong path, so I applied and was approved. Later, I realized how prized this committee was; it turned out to be very important to the promotion and tenure process. Graduate faculty status was looked upon very highly at Alcorn; he knew this, but I didn't. I am forever grateful to him for helping me prepare in this way. Today, I enjoy teaching graduate students as well as undergraduates and I was able to become a thesis advisor and co-advisor because of my membership. This had a positive impact on my institution as well, as I was able to assist over twelve graduate students in either the Biology or Biotechnology Master's programs to complete requirements for graduation. What a gift to be able to give to young people and to the University.

My graduate advisor, Dr. George Wilson, at the University of Kansas (KU) was also an important mentor to me when I began my career at Alcorn. We kept in touch and worked very hard to put together an article based in part on my dissertation work. I did not get an opportunity to publish any research work while I was in graduate school at KU. However, Dr. Wilson assured me that we would get something published. He kept his word, and in 2006, I could finally say that I had co-authored a peer-reviewed research article. In a way, I was grateful that the publication came later because I was able to put the name of Alcorn State University on the article.

Still others helped me prepare early on in my career as well. Dr. Cynthia Larive, one of my former instructors at KU, got me involved with the ASDL (Analytical Sciences Digital Library) group. At first, I was unsure if this group was for me because I did not see any African-Americans like myself. However, the group made me feel a part of the team and valued right away; I knew that I had found a place in which I could flourish. I am now a contributing associate editor and serve as a facilitator training others to use active learning in their analytical chemistry courses. This connection has had an even broader impact on my profession and my institution. In 2016, Alcorn was awarded an NSF (National Science Foundation) grant, for which I serve as project director, to infuse active learning into the STEM curriculum of courses in Chemistry, Physics, Biological Sciences, Mathematics, and Computer Science. We have seen great success in student learning outcomes during the first year of the grant. With this grant we were also able to further the goals of the Chemistry and Physics Department toward obtaining ACS (American Chemical Society) approval of the chemistry program by purchasing modern equipment (HPLC and FTIR). The students and faculty at Alcorn have benefited greatly from this grant, and I am very grateful to have had the opportunity to provide this to them and to build capacity in the Chemistry and Physics department, The School of Arts and Sciences, and Alcorn State University.

Service was an area that had always come natural to me. Immediately upon taking the position at Alcorn, I began to work with the Biotechnology summer program providing hands-on training in biotechnology to area high school teachers and students. This service afforded me the opportunity to get to know the community stakeholders and their needs. I realized that the community needed Alcorn to be a beacon of hope and continue to bridge knowledge gaps that existed for both teachers and students. I believe that this experience really made me become more aware of where my true passion and destiny lied: uplifting the STEM knowledge base of the Alcorn community. I realized that I was being called to serve beyond the chemistry department. Since then, I have joined many committees that I feel my expertise could be useful: academic advisor, SACS reaffirmation of accreditation writer, QEP (Quality Enhancement Plan) program assessment, IRB (Institutional Review Board), Faculty Senate, and School of Arts and Sciences Advancement and Alumni Liaison. I am especially proud of the work that the Advancement Liaison team did in leading efforts on the first Faculty and Staff Giving Campaign in 2017; during this campaign, we were able to motivate faculty and staff to support student scholarships and we raised a significant amount within a few months.

Never stop learning and improving yourself

I believe that a successful person realizes that if she is going to make an impact, she must not settle where she is and rest on her laurels. I can say that I have never felt that I had arrived, even after I obtained full professorship.

When opportunities that seemed like a challenge presented themselves, I was not afraid to take them on and learn along the way. One such opportunity was the Biotechnology Masters Program. I accepted the opportunity to lead the effort to develop this interdisciplinary program. Through this endeavor, I was able to make new alliances, and I believe that I unknowingly gained the respect of many colleagues. This experience taught me how to communicate and work through differences. In 2014, one of my colleagues, Dr. Yolanda Jones, and I were selected to participate in the PCFF (Preparing Critical Faculty for the Future) project. This project taught me invaluable skills: high impact teaching methods, ways to be more effective, how to network, and how to survive as a women of color in the STEM profession, just to name a few. I believe that this program also spearheaded my interest in administration. Later, I was accepted into the OURS (Opportunity for UnderRepresented Scholars) Program, which I feel gave me the tools and practical training that I needed to be confident and prepared to become a University leader. The Chemistry and Physics Department is still working on the ALP (action learning project), which is to gain approval of the chemistry program by the ACS. The negotiation skills that I learned helped position me to communicate with the administration in an effective way and garner their trust and support of our accreditation efforts. Today, we are closer than we have ever been to our goal of ACS approval of our chemistry program. The training that I received in the OURS program has also allowed me to better communicate with and supervise faculty. The program helped me to realize my strengths and weaknesses so that I could continue to improve on the weaknesses, while continuing to use my strengths for the benefit of my institution.

While serving as a Research Assistant Professor at Alcorn State University, I tried to do all that I could to improve myself. I enrolled in certificate courses to strengthen my research skills, I attended workshops to improve my grant writing skills, and I got involved in many activities and committees at the institution. I joined the faculty senate, Institutional Review Board (serving as Chair from 2014-2016), graduate faculty, and many other committees. Joining these committees allowed me to meet new people and make important connections, which would lead to future collaborations. It also allowed me to broaden my horizons to better understand how different University components worked to benefit the students. I gained a better appreciation for how I could work with others to impact my institution.

Find that thing that makes you tick and nurture it despite the obstacles

This is the thing that you'd do without pay and be satisfied. I believe that too many people are trying to live the dreams of others; therefore, they are dissatisfied with their careers. I believe that when we discover our true passion and follow it, we all can prosper and impact others in a positive way. At first I wanted to be a pharmacist or medical doctor because I did not want to be poor all my life. I had been told that these fields were the way to go. I quickly learned that I did not want to do these things. I also thought that I wanted to be a research scientist and work for a major company; however, I was a natural at teaching, and oral and written communication came easy to me. So, why was I ignoring my natural abilities? This reality hit hard when I interviewed with a big chemical company and the interviewer put his legs across the desk in front of me. This was the sign, I was told, that you just got dissed. At that point, I knew the chemical industry was not for me. When my undergraduate advisor told me about the opportunity at Alcorn with the Biotechnology Center, I looked into it. I said, why not give it a try. It was a research position, but with the option to teach and obtain tenure. So, I applied and got invited for an interview. I was very excited when I got the position. Things were okay for the first year or so. However, soon I started feeling isolated and inadequate. I remember struggling to have my voice heard among what seemed at the time smarter more experienced men. Being a natural introvert seemed to make things worse. There were times when I thought that I would lose it. However, I decided that I would fight with all my might to be progressive. I took on the community service activities working with community high school teachers and students, providing them hands-on training in biotechnology techniques. I did the day-to-day work with them. This program lasted for three years, and each year, I made sure to do my best to make the program better each year. What I didn't realize at the time was that I was making a connection with the community that would serve me well in future endeavors. I accepted the opportunity to serve as the major advisor to the first graduate student. Even though I had a small child at the time, I worked extra hard to train him. This led to the first publication of the Biotechnology Center. It was not easy to do because there were those who did not want me to be the first author and some who did not want the publication to be successful at all. I later found out that there was someone who did not want me to get tenure (someone actually wrote a letter against me). Someone also did not want me to get the same salary as my colleagues, despite the fact that I had a Ph.D. just as they did and postdoctoral training on top of the Ph.D., which many of them did not have. Finding these things out made me angry at first, but I decided that I would not let my anger affect my performance. I had to channel that anger into something positive. I decided that I would use this as a motivation to push myself to be excellent at everything that I could. I took on challenges, especially if I thought it would benefit the community or students. I volunteered to lead the efforts to establish an interdisciplinary Master's degree Program in Biotechnology. Even though it took a few years before the program was officially established, I am very proud to have made a significant contribution to this program, which is still going strong today.

My passion is STEM education. No matter if I am providing training to Middle school students, high school students, undergraduates, or graduate students, I have a passion for educating students about various STEM fields. When you are passionate about what you do, others will take notice because you will naturally give your best and enjoy doing it. I allowed my passion to continue to lead me and as a result was nominated to apply for professional development to participate in PCFF and OURS programs, which provided professional development training in STEM education and STEM leadership, respectively. Both programs had a significant impact on my skills and leadership abilities in the STEM area, which in turn, had a significant impact on my promotion to full professor. In 2011, I was awarded the H.E.A.D.W.A.E. (Higher Education Appreciation Day, Working for Academic Excellence) Outstanding Faculty Honoree award from the Mississippi Legislature.

Have a strong spiritual life and sense of purpose beyond your life

Almost as long as I can remember, I have had a strong spiritual life. I know that God has a purpose for my life. It took a while for me to figure out what I was supposed to be doing. However, nurturing my spiritual relationship has allowed me to be able to be led into my destiny. This may sound like a cliché, but it is how I truly feel. I believe that my purpose is to allow God to show his faithfulness and goodness to others through my life. I don't believe this is because I have been so good...far from it. It is hard to explain how I came to this conclusion. However, God has revealed it to me over time, and I have become much calmer and unafraid to take risks. It was as if I did not give much thought to what others thought of me. My goal (and destiny) is not defined by people, but by God. When I was going through the motions and not taking my relationship with God very seriously, I was miserable. I hated going to work and I complained a lot. However, after allowing God to take His place at the forefront of my thoughts, my attitude and performance improved greatly. Now, I take time to strengthen my spiritual life and listen to God's voice as he leads me through tough times and steers me away at other times. I have come to realize that I am not supposed to be protected from every situation, but that God has allowed me to go through some things to make me stronger and wiser.

In everything that you do, make time to hear from God and nurture your relationship with Him. I have found that it was not enough to just go to service on Sunday. I needed a day-to-day relationship that would help me face my enemies (who were all around me) and wanted to see me fail. God has provided wisdom beyond measure that I am very careful to attribute to Him. He has allowed me to see things coming and head them off before they hit. Other things he has allowed me to experience, but for a reason. At times we need strength that is superhuman; this is the strength that only God can provide. There was a time in my life when I had to endure many back-to-back board complaints; at the same time, I lost a beloved faculty member, and I struggled with finances. At first, I thought I would lose my mind, but going through these obstacles actually forced me to let go of my own life and place my life in God's hands. Not only did he bring me through, he brought me out on the other side with a smile, content heart, and better finances than I have ever had in my life. Today, I am able to face those who plot against me and tough situations because I understand that I stand not on my own strength, but on the shoulders of my God! Every day I wake with a renewed sense of purpose and thankfulness for where I am in life. I don't believe that I would have made it to full professorship if I had not been able to get beyond challenging things that had happened to me and embraced my purpose.

Surround yourself with a support system and put on your armour

Times will get very tough in this profession. Sometimes it will be hard to get beyond something that happens to you. This is the time when a support system is crucial. This support system must be people that you trust to be completely honest with you. If you need constructive criticism, they don't mind giving it to you. However, if you need someone to listen to you vent for half an hour, he or she will do that too. Be cautious though, in the selection of your support system. Sometimes we can think that someone is a member of our support system when he or she really wants to be close to you so that he or she can know what is going on with you and stab you in the back. Take time to get to know people before you let them into your support system. I made the mistake of letting one faculty member into my support system too early own. He would pretend to be helping me, but was stabbing me in the back all along. He was making me feel that he cared about me and my success, but when he was in the presence of other faculty, he was bad mouthing me. It took me a few years to figure him out, but I immediately let him go. I had to go outside my unit to find a colleague who was genuine and gave me honest, sound advice. Now, whenever I am thinking of doing something major, I seek the advice from my support system. The people in my support system include my husband, Clinton, my sisters (Sheila, Alecia, Brenda, and Lesa), a few colleagues, my dean, and several mentors, including Dr. Beverly O'Bryant, Dr. Joseph Russell, and Dr. Troy Stewart. I don't always seek advice from everyone. There are certain areas that I speak to certain members about. However, if you have no support system, it could be difficult to make any significant changes at your institution. Your support system will be honest with you and help you to stay grounded. There have been times when I have been blind to certain situations and individuals in my support system have helped me to see things from a more practical viewpoint.

There was a point in my career when I was getting one ethics line complaint after the other; I believe I received around eight in less than a one year time span. It was obvious that someone was out to destroy me. At first, it really hurt me deeply. I had trouble eating and focusing for a few months. During this same time, I was dealing with the death of a beloved faculty member. It took all that I had to face the students and the faculty and be strong for them. However, I decided that I had made it through some tough times in the past and that I was not about to give in now. I purposed to focus on the good that was going on and the things that I was grateful for each day. I had to overshadow the bad with good. I had to change my mindset in order to face these difficult obstacles that tried to suck the life out of my career. Instead of directing my thoughts day after day toward the negative things going on at the time, I directed my thoughts toward positive things; I began writing on a National Science Foundation (NSF) STEM teaching grant, working more seriously toward accreditation of the chemistry program, and writing a publication on STEM learning in the area of Bioanalytical Chemistry. The malicious attacks began in late 2015. Today, in 2017, I have received the NSF funding that I was seeking and two additional grants, published the book chapter, and we are closer than ever before to gaining accreditation for our chemistry program. The lesson that I learned is that we should not desire to stop obstacles from getting in our way, instead, we should turn obstacles into opportunities to excel or opportunities for our faith to shine through. It is in those dark times that we are made stronger. For how many of us get stronger without something to push us to be stronger. I realized that if I was going to get to the next level in my career, I had to be able to handle hard criticism and even out right maliciousness. This is when I lived the quote "higher level, more devils." Dr. Thomas Bolden told me that I had to toughen up and I did. Today, I am much stronger because of my support system and because I realize that obstacles are sometimes necessary in order to grow us and test our endurance.

**Don't say yes to everything, so that you can
be effective at more things**

Developing oneself takes time. It will not happen overnight. It takes hard work, commitment, and wisdom to know what to say no to and what to say yes to. I made this statement because many times we as professional women get stuck doing the things that don't count toward promotion and/or tenure, and in some cases beyond the immediate gratification of the person who asked. Of course, most of us love to serve and our motherly instincts makes us want to save the world. However, for our progression in academia and for our sanity, I add, we must not take on the world. We must be smart about our decisions to do certain things. After being taken a few times and obtaining a little wisdom, I stopped to ask questions before I took on tasks: Who is going to benefit from this activity? How much of my time is this going to take? Will this activity be helpful or harmful to me? These three questions were key to me deciding what I was willing to take on. Believe me, once people realize that you will work hard and be committed to do your best, everything under the sun will come your way. There will be no shortage of opportunities for most. However, in many cases you will need to decide if it is worth it. Keep in mind that there are some things that you must do, or you will be in bad with your supervisor. But those things that tend to come your way because you are the one who can and will get it done, take a close look at those things. I have been taken in the past by writing up someone else work or communicating my ideas and finding that they were later taken by someone. Avoid allowing others to use you for their gain. There is a difference between collaboration and being out right used. If you are unsure if you should take on a task, consulting your mentors may help. In my current position as chair, I find myself in consultation when I need advice. There are those who have walked a similar path and can help you when you need advice.

Summary

I began my academic career at Alcorn State University as a research professor of biotechnology in 2001. While serving in this capacity, I led efforts to establish the Master's in Biotechnology Program. I advised the graduate student, Peter Bate, who published the first research article for the Program. The research also won the First Place Poster Award at the ARD meeting in 2006. In 2007, I joined the Chemistry and Physics Department as an assistant professor of chemistry. I immersed myself in teaching, research, and service. I received the Professor of the year award in 2007 and co-initiated the Departmental Undergraduate Research Group with my colleague, Dr. Yolanda Jones in 2010. We trained many undergraduates, who presented their research at professional conferences. We were awarded many research grants, totalling over 2 million dollars. Funding agencies included the USDA, NIH, DOH, Thurgood Marshall, and the NSF. I was promoted to associate professor (with tenure) in 2009. A total of four peer-reviewed publications were published from 2010 to 2016. In 2013, I served as Interim Chair of the Chemistry and Physics Department; in 2014, I was promoted to permanent Chair. In 2017, I was promoted to full professor. As Professor and Chair of the Department, I still engage in teaching, research, and service to my institution.

CHAPTER 5

Advancing Yourself Advances Your Students
Bianca Garner, PhD

The importance of having role models cannot be overstated. When children are growing up, they need those individuals who can encourage them to be more and do more. Children need to see individuals who have achieved success and have these people engage them. The connection of having someone who is successful believe in you can make all of the difference in whether people buckle during challenges or soar. I have always felt privileged to have strong female role models to guide me. From my mother and maternal grandmother, to my counselors and teachers, I always was surrounded by strong women who pushed me to be better. They were critical, but supportive. They were firm, but kind. They wanted me to reach my full potential and always saw more in me than I saw in myself. While they might not have had doctoral degrees, their positions of importance provided me the support I needed.

It was this type of support that propelled me to attend a Historically Black College and University (HBCU). My experience was filled with incredible opportunities. Not because I might have been the number one student, but because I never placed limitations on myself. The support I received prior allowed me to handle any challenges that I faced. I was never afraid someone would say no to me, nor was I concerned about others impression if I did not receive the award or the internship. I was keenly aware, however, that there were few African-Americans professors in the science disciplines. I knew then that given the opportunity, I would return to an HBCU to be a person who could serve as a mentor for students who might not have had the type of support I did.

I always kept in mind that I wanted to be the motivator for a new generation of students. I had few women of color faculty members and wanted to share my motivation and experiences with them. As with many, it was not a straight line for my tenure track appointment. I was a postdoctoral researcher, taught adjunct classes and worked as a consultant. Regardless, I always kept in mind that my end goal was to teach and mentor underrepresented students. Every decision that I made was always done so with consideration for how it would assist me in obtaining a professorial position.

Thus, when I received a tenure track appointment for an Associate Professor of Biology, I was thrilled. My goal was to teach and mentor students. Nothing more. Simply attain a faculty position and begin my blissful life as a support system for underrepresented students. Research? No thank you. Committee assignments? Only a few. Tenure? I have to, so okay. Promotion? No thank you.

I simply wanted to work with students and assist them in any way that I could. Thus, I began teaching and working on programs to help increase the graduate school pipeline for students. I worked on committees because they helped me to support the students. There was never an intentional plan on how I worked. I only knew that committee assignments were necessary for me to assist with student opportunities. The research grants that I supported, provided financial support for students who would never have had the opportunity to engage in research.

This can become a common theme for women in higher education. We work on ideas and projects not necessarily for ourselves but for the benefits provided to the institution. This is also, unfortunately, where many women tend to stay. There is a certain level of satisfaction at these levels, where you are achieving success in the mission of helping students. As with many people, I enjoyed the job and was not concerned about advancing. Finding joy and happiness in academia is a double edged sword. You become comfortable and familiar with what you are doing. There is success in watching students grow and reach their potential. You find the "ah-ha" moments particularly invigorating during tough times. The best are those moments when students begin to speak with their colleagues about the importance of studying or planning. These are the goals that keep many people, especially women of color, stained in one place. While there are challenges with people and administrators, there is always the impact that we have on the students that continue to motivate us to continue on. This, however, is one of the main reasons why we should advance. If representation is truly important, why is it okay for women of color to not apply for promotion or tenure? If we want our students to always go beyond what they think are limitations or challenges, why do we not wish to go further as well?

This realization did not come readily. Because I wanted to expose myself to information that could help my students, I applied for and received a leadership training fellowship. It was there that I first learned that women and women of color are less likely to advance beyond the Associate Professor level. It was not that women were working less, they were just not advancing beyond that particular level. I thought of my own institution and realized that no women of color had advanced to full professor in the sciences. There were capable women of color who could have advanced. They worked hard and were engaged in their community. Still, this was not important to them and was not their focus.

I began to wonder how or if it impacts students, who see faculty members at intuitions for long periods of time without advancement? When we consider how important representation is, shouldn't all women be pushing the envelope to gain tenure or be promoted? This in no way indicates that there will not be challenges that are inherent to the system as well as the individual intuitions. I was hired as an untenured Associate Professor. I was very vocal during meetings and knew that some tenured faculty who could decide my fate were not pleased. All institutions have these kinds of issues, whereby there may be built in biases against you. Does that mean we should not try to advance as high as we should?

I realized at that training session that I was not working towards advancement. I was doing the work, so when did I get to the point where it was okay for me to limit myself and not try. I have never allowed my students to take the easy way when faced with a challenge, so why wasn't I working toward a goal that should be available for all faculty. That moment was life changing as I realized that it was as much for myself as it was for my students. I had to work toward advancement. Nothing is guaranteed and advancing myself would provide me with support should I need to leave the institution. It would also make me a stronger voice for the students I served. That experience and the revelations I received changed my whole approach to how I live professionally.

I became intentional in identifying programs that would help me advance. I did not focus solely on promotion and tenure, but I focused on what were the professional and personal gains that I would receive from the activities. As I had done at Xavier University of Louisiana, I applied to any and every opportunity for training. It would have been easy to dismiss some of the opportunities because of issues that I could not change. Tougaloo College is a liberal arts institution, with no graduate students. Regardless, I applied for research grants and research fellowships. Instead of just participating on committee assignments, I accepted positions of leadership on the committees. I didn't anticipate any job opportunities, other than those that would increase my competitiveness for tenure and promotion.

I reviewed the handbook to examine exactly what the criteria were for both promotion and tenure. Whereas before, I knew it was a possibility, I had never really planned for the process and thus had never taken the time to investigate exactly what was required. I reviewed the process and examined where I was with each of the criteria. It was a challenge, as I had never kept up my curriculum vitae or kept track of the awards I had received. In many cases, I never even mentioned those awards to Tougaloo faculty members. In one of my training sessions, this was clearly identified as a weakness area. Because I never wanted to advance, I never conveyed the successes that I was having. This changed! As I prepared for the review process, I found every letter, every person, every drop of evidence to support that I was invested in the college.

There were a number individuals whom suggested I would have no problems with tenure and promotion. While I felt support from this, I never counted on promotion and tenure as a guarantee. This is a mistake that often we fall in. Because of the good works we do on committees or in the laboratory, we might assume that "we got this". I always felt that this was the wrong attitude faculty members take. I would never allow my students to feel so confident that they would pass without doing the work.

In the end, I did receive both tenure and promotion. When I applied, I knew that I had done everything that I could to make myself a good candidate. I also knew that my students were watching. They knew when I was promoted. They knew when I received more responsibilities. They talked with me about the leadership training opportunities, always asking what my trips were like. They knew and counted on me assisting them if given the opportunity.

It is true that we cannot do everything. We must, however, do all that we can to move the needle of the number of female faculty members who attain tenure and promotion. Our students need us to move. Our communities need us to move. Our institutions need us to advance. Most importantly, we as women need to advance.

CHAPTER 6

Praying and Praising Through Challenging Situations

Carolyn Bingham Howard, PhD

Mentor from the Master

When selected by my departmental peers to chair an ad-hoc committee established to recommend supplemental criteria within my College, the College of Science, Engineering and Technology (CSET), I gladly accepted, just as I had done for other "special" committees since my hire. I took my job seriously, since I was a proud, first-generation graduate of the same HBCU I came back to work for, the only university where I have ever worked. To my amazement and dismay, though the supplemental criteria suggested by our ad-hoc committee had not yet been universally approved, it was the standard my portfolio was measured against. I had far exceeded the University's criteria, but my packet did not measure up to the elevated standard of the CSET supplemental criteria. I emphasized the fact that the criteria "one" is hired under should be the same they are judged by for promotion. My best efforts and arguments failed so it seemed that everything had worked against me, including me. I was denied promotion to Full Professor and I was livid. How dare they make me lead noose-woman to fortify the noose used to hang myself! I stormed down the hall, down the stairs, and up the next hall, but just before I turned the last corner leading to my Chair's office, I vividly remembered what my pastor said, "*Always go up before you go off*". I stepped into the ladies room to pray and to collect myself. I prayed the word of God, *The LORD is my shepherd; I shall not want. He maketh me to lie down in green pastures: He leadeth me beside the still waters. He restoreth my soul: He leadeth me in the paths of righteousness for His name's sake"* (Psalms 23:1-3).

Then, I went in to ask my Chair for an explanation as to why the promotion criterion used to evaluate my dossier was different than the one used University-wide, the one used for others in my department that had been promoted, and even for another candidate who sought promotion along with me. I was told that the mandate had come from CSET leadership and it was being used with my packet since I had led the effort in developing the CSET supplemental criterion. Realizing that this situation was bigger than me, (... *for His name's sake*), because of my love for JSU and for fear of being identified as "an angry black women", I accepted my fate and decided to try again the following year. After *three years* of failed attempts to reach the benchmarks set forth in the new CSET Supplemental Criteria for Promotion and Tenure, and seeing every other male colleague in my department promoted, incidentally, all who were hired after me, I made a decision to make it a deliberate practice in my life to pray and to praise God before taking any actions, ever. Before beginning to assemble my dossier for a fourth time, I sought the Lord and prayed His Holy Word, "Psalm 23: Yea, though I walk through the valley of the shadow of death, I will fear no evil: for Thou art with me; Thy rod and Thy staff they comfort me. Thou preparest a table before me in the presence of mine enemies: Thou anointest my head with oil; my cup runneth over. Surely goodness and mercy shall follow me all the days of my life: and I will dwell in the house of The LORD forever" (Psalm 23:4-6).

After spending time before The Lord, I opted not to apply for promotion the following year and soon after entered into collaboration with a female colleague at another institution, a brilliant and confident woman I met at a cancer research meeting. She was intrigued by my work and became a faithful consultant and my research collaborator. We not only worked well together when I traveled to her state-of-the art research facility, we wrote funded grants and published together. I had never experience such connectivity and this boosted my productivity. On top of that, after hours, since she and her husband invited me to live with them and their family at their home instead of a hotel each time I travelled there, I felt free to share with her about the racial and gender inequities in STEM at my beloved alma mater. She became more than just a collaborator; she was my mentor and helped me to understand that overcoming my reluctance to speak out for fear of potential consequences was my greatest hindrance in my progression from Associate to Full Professor, not the quality of my work. As a result, I was able to push past hurdles of self-doubt, anger, judgement and false burdens. I stood in my decision to make each day a day wherein I prayed, praised God and persistently strived to reach this pinnacle achieved by only an alarmingly low number of female, African-American PhDs. Although I have not found a sponsor (Ibarra, Carter, & Silva, 2010), I did find a mentor and I was promoted to Full Professor.

Shooting Blanks

I will now rewind to simpler times in the Academy. As a child of The King, wife, mother of 6, grandmother of 7, tenured Associate Professor of Biology, Sunday school teacher, etc., I had led peo-

73

ple, from those that were very young to highly educated or well-trained grown folks. Consistently, I had worn all these "leader" hats, seeking to "protect and support" not "direct and micro-manage." I thought I had it all together with this covert leadership style, gaining followership without bending to favoritism or falling into schisms. I routinely put out fires to correct any errors while letting people be people, causing them to willingly comply with my requests, with my "sanctified self". I felt fulfilled and had mastered many skills, so I believed I had obtained true work-life balance (Barsh & Cranston, 2011). However, I heard my pastor say, "A person's perception is their truth and that which they perceive as true remains their truth until they encounter a greater truth".

The greater truth that I encountered as I sought the highest academic rank, Full Professor, is taught sense has its place of value, but bought sense is immeasurable. This process became a major turning point in my life, affording me sense bought at high cost. Outside of the workplace, I was valued and respected. After all, I had made it through my PhD program as a divorced mother of three, did a one-year post-doc, landed a job as a college professor at the same beloved university where I received my BS degree, had moved up the ranks from Assistant to Associate, and was tenured. Besides, I was a go-getter and was very opinionated, character traits I believed brought added value. Yet, no words of validation pertaining to me, well accomplished in my own rights, came out of my workplace. None came from the powerful men holding on to the popular mindset of solidified bureaucratic rule, especially since influences from men from cultures which all but marginalize women weighed heavily into the culture and climate associated with organizational leadership in CSET, an ideology echoed by Eagly and Carli (2007). In a battle where I felt men in power were shooting missiles of isolation, inequity, implicit and explicit biases, and disrespect, all I could muster up as a defense was an utterly beautiful and flawless outer appearance seeping harmless blanks wrapped in thin casings. I was expected to be tough skinned, confident, balanced and unmovable, yet I was wounded and scorned, lacking reinforcements of support and mentoring. Through it all, I refused to be timid and to say and do whatever the higher ups wanted said and done to fit their selfish agendas and planned scenarios. Years went by wherein I received neither promotion nor merit-based pay raises. Yet, my values did not allow me to go along with things I saw as morally and logistically wrong. Labeled as not being a team player, I became an outcast, refusing to be part of the various silos of people tending to provide strong support for each other and rewarding one another. This continued until my God and my research paired me with my external collaborator who became my mentor. What was the worst thing that could happen, I wouldn't get promoted? LOL! I held on to the resolve that promotion does not come from the north, the south, the east nor the west, but it comes from above. I knew my gift will make room for me and bring me before great kings. This invoked me to strive even harder to change my challenging situations into victories. It was comforting and encouraging, knowing that although the struggle was constant and intense, initiatives like JSU Advance and the OURS program were made available to me as I sought to right the ship and obtain the rank of Full Professor.

"Journaling changes one's perception of how time is best spent."
Carolyn B. Howard

Advancement Via JSU Advance

The day I started to journal at my first JSU Advance Summer Writing Retreat, I got the revelation that I will oftentimes be judged by how I spend my time. A situation comes to mind related to management of the Animal Core Facility at my university. I did the leg work and invested countless hours toward having our outdated animal room renovated and the renovations were completed under my watch. But, with the very next funding cycle, I was replaced as manager by a male colleague who was hired after the newly renovated facility was already up and running. He was given accolades and was promoted to Full Professor while I remained an Associate Professor for several years afterwards. Though Eagly and Carli (2007) described this sort of situation and I continued to pray and praise, I found it very difficult to advance at my institution. At times it seemed near impossible for me to meet the extreme time demands, and double standards requiring more from women than men, coupled with few self-advantages. Nevertheless, I was not ignorant. The bible says, "*in all your getting, get understanding*". I understood I needed to be 1) bold, 2) unafraid to take risks, and 3) accountable; and by no means stand idly by as someone else took credit for my accomplishments. My efforts had to be documented, journaled about, and reflected in my dossier.

I redeemed the time by establishing some ground control. Regardless of how demanding the job became, and we all know some days are better than others, I found a way to balance work with family and church responsibilities. I journaled each morning, meditated, set clear priorities, devised a time-management schedule allowing some flexibility and down-time, and stayed prayed up. These things helped me stay grounded and I could still factor in "me-time". At first, priority setting was the one thing that caused me to be out of balance and was at the root of my problems in meeting the demands and responsibilities of career, community and society, family and self. Another big mistake I tended to make was being busy, but not being effective, finding myself doing a good job and succeeding at the wrong things. Journaling caused me to focus my time, energy and attention toward decision making and my discipline toward finding my God given purpose, not being confronted with the challenge of not knowing what to do. Matthew 6:33 says, "Seek ye first the kingdom of God and His righteousness and all these things will be added unto you". So, I kept and continue to keep the main thing the main thing. I first find out what God's priorities are and putting those things first, I avoid the greatest tragedy of life, life without purpose. I am now rooted and grounded in the Word of God, so I don't have to row so hard in order to put first things first and maintain balance.

OURS Preparation

The Opportunities for UnderRepresented Scholars (OURS) Program has prepared me, along with other women of color, for academic leadership positions (Engerman and Luster-Teasley, Editors, 2017). OURS Program affiliations, along with self-discipline and self-examination, and taking responsibility for self-development all factored into my move in rank to Full Professor. I learned from past mistakes and made necessary adjustments to come up to the task. Now when I recognize a future opportunity, and it is time to dust my feet off and move to another establishment, organization or area, I will do so with confidence and intentionality. Not every work environment is a good fit for everyone. Although I believe my path has helped to change the climate at our institution, if the men remain too stiff-necked and refuse to allow women to advance into leadership roles, there are certainly other places to venture. The OURS Program experience has had a more powerful influence upon me toward shaping me as an aspiring leader than any other event or series of events in my life thus far. I am a member of a select group of women of color. Not only am I a Full Professor, but I am also an effective leader. I have a set standard for hard work at my university, I am prepared and productive, I prioritize all aspects of life and develop and execute plans that reflect those priorities, and I stand to bring added value to any place within any space I occupy.

What Is Valued

When we can experience things and share them or we can learn from others' experiences, it is possible to use that knowledge and not let ourselves walk into the same brick walls. Life is far too short to experience everything. The challenge is to understand ourselves well enough to discover where we can use our gifts to serve others. I will go on to say that it was important to me to reflect upon the BIBLE (Basic Instructions Before Leaving Earth), and allow it to continue to transform me into that which He has called me to be. Jeremiah 1:5 says, "Before I formed you in the womb I knew you; Before you were born I sanctified you; I ordained you a prophet to the nations". Also Philippians 1:6 states, "Being confident of this very thing, that He who has begun a good work in you will complete it until the day of Jesus Christ". The Holy Spirit is my guide. Since God foreknew me and His Spirit guides me, I can't help but be authentically me. However, when we see others take a particular path and succeed well, we must be mindful and careful not to turn into a copycat of them. One person's path probably wouldn't make the next person succeed. Additionally, real authenticity doesn't allow anyone to try to imitate someone else. People see right through that facade and lose trust for you when you are not genuine and authentic, but instead are attempting to be a replica of someone else. An old ad campaign slogan came to mind, "Inquiring minds want to know. I want to know". So if you really want to know how I have succeeded against the odds, I would sum it all up by saying that there is no magic formula for success. Instead, I have found real value in relationships and lessons learned from experiences, allowing success to emerge from the life I have been blessed to live – bought sense.

At Last

It has been said that the second time around is so much better than the first time, so imagine how much better the fourth time submitting my dossier for promotion to Full Professor must have been. Aside from praying, praising, finding a mentor, licking my wounds and being healed from the inside out, getting my priorities straight and getting all my ducks in a row, I believe patience and persistence paid off for me. Galatians 6:9 states, "And let us not be weary in well doing: for in due season we shall reap, if we faint not". During the year between my third and fourth (the successful one) submissions, I served on the College Promotion and Tenure Committee and evaluated portfolios submitted by my colleagues seeking tenure and promotion to the rank of Associate Professor, two important benchmarks I had already reached. Also, I attended promotion and tenure preparation workshops to pick up any particular nuggets that had eluded me for several years and sought recommendation letters from 1) a student that had taken my Microbiology class, 2) an undergraduate research student, 3) a graduate student I had mentored in my Breast Cancer Research Laboratory, 4) my research mentor, 5) one of my colleagues, and 6) the leader of a certain public service organization I have been a part of and worked within for over 25 years. Each person reflected upon the impact I had made on their lives and suddenly I realized that my life has truly had meaning. Relationships are the best thing we have going in the earth. The relationships I have been blessed to forge and the work I love have come together in such a rewarding way that it became less important to prove anything to anyone and much more important to live day to day, from those days forward, with a grateful heart full of joy, peace and love, the greatest of these three, love. I became more confident and relaxed at the same time, and instead of trying to convince others of how hard I had worked, I allowed the love for what I have do, and the lives I have touched speak throughout the pages of my promotion packets. It made all the difference, and I am now a different person than I was when I began this quest over five years ago. At last I can say as said in Romans 12:2, "And be not conformed to this world: but be ye transformed by the renewing of your mind, that ye may prove what is that good, and acceptable, and perfect, will of God". Before such time, I was not fit to be a Full Professor, nor was I fit for The Master's use. But now I am, thus I am. It is my fervent prayer that anyone experiencing similar or even totally different challenges compared to mine will find hope and encouragement from my recounting my experiences and press forward to your own success.

References

Barsh, J. & Cranston, S. (2011). *How Remarkable Women Lead: The Breakthrough Model for Work and Life.* Crown Business: New York.

Eagly, A.H. & Carli, L. (2007). *Through the Labyrinth: The Truth about How Women Become Leaders* (pp.137-160). Harvard Business School Press: Boston.

Engerman & Luster-Teasley, Ed. (2017). *Women Called To Lead.* Fielding University Press, Fielding Graduate University: California.

Ibarra, H., Carter, N. M., & Silva, C. (2011). "Why men still get more promotions than women." *Harvard Business Review*, 80-85.

CHAPTER 7

Navigating from the Nexus: My Journey and Impact

Tonya Smith-Jackson, PhD, CPE

The word "nexus" summarizes my overall experience moving through the professorial ranks, because it seems to be exactly where I found myself --- in the middle, at the intersections, belonging to and connecting many things. Yet, I sometimes felt like I did not belong to a specific "tribe", except my own family, that is. Indeed, the process from assistant professor to full professor places many of us in the position of navigating a multiplicity of tribes. Code-switching on multiple contextual levels is an effective tool. Code-switching initially referred to the psycholinguistics of changing speech acts and nonverbal behavior based on the social context, such as changing from "main-stream English" to Black English Vernacular (Heller, 1988). The concept has been extended to incorporate cross-cultural code-switching, where individuals alter how they socially engage within "culturally ingrained systems of behavior (Molinsky, 2007, p. 623)." So, before discussing the pathway to full professor, I need to discuss context. Before doing so, I summarize the experience as ultimately leading to my point of view on the impact I have made thus far at the HBCU, North Carolina A&T State University (NCA&T), where I have served as a Department Chair since 2013. These impacts fall into three main areas that underpin my commitment and enthusiasm for NC A&T:

1.   Confronting bigotry in the scholarly arena.
2.   Neither apologizing for who I am, nor assimilating.
3.   Being real; being authentic.

Tribes have cultures and customs that influence what and how people think. These tribes challenge our own identities and world views. Thank goodness I grew up with a Dad who was a career Air Force enlisted man, and a Mom who was in no way afraid of living anywhere on the globe, in spite of living at the poverty line with six kids. My parents talked about different tribal ways of thinking and helped us understand that tribes drive how people behave and how they treat others, especially those who are external to the tribe. As a result, I had many experiences that influenced and often challenged my tribal world view, but I understood other tribes brought different perspectives. Traveling in the military had a strong effect on how I saw and understood things; and ultimately, my need to get to full professor rank because I wanted to have credibility to challenge some of these tribal world views, especially those perpetuated by the tribes with the most power and privilege. It began in the military.

The military masks poverty very well; you can always go to family services to get food and you will never be homeless (rent is low or no cost). Being a military family afforded certain experiences free of charge or at very discounted prices. These experiences included immersion in highly diverse cultures with direct exposure to schools, languages, customs, religions, food, and, unfortunately, biases and bigotry. At one point, we lived in a tiny, unmercifully cold, mobile home in North Dakota, because no one would rent to my Father. He would call on the phone to verify that something was available, only to show up at the prospective landlord's door step to be told it was no longer available. This was code for "We don't rent to Black people." The Air Force, who subsidized and supported landlords to rent homes to military families, did nothing to assist my Father, and was, in some ways, complicit with these forms of discrimination. I don't think my Father ever forgave North Dakota for how he was treated. At another point, we lived in the Philippines in "so-called" Air Force family housing. It was hot, ant and lizard infested. Now that I look back on it, the paint that was peeling from the walls in our house was probably lead paint. But, my parents, no matter what, could not be stopped from taking advantage of every opportunity that lay before them. They took no excuses from us. Education was the only way out. We had one rule - when you graduate from high school, you can either join the military or go to college. One way or the other, you had to take the steps to make your own way. They gave us the tools to do it, so, no excuses would be accepted.

Two years before my Father retired from the Air Force, we returned to North Carolina. We started farming and growing cucumbers for a pickle company. Needless to say, the work was hard, hot, and brutal on the back and knees. Two years after that, having received my acceptance letter to attend the North Carolina School of Science and Mathematics (NCSSM) in Durham, NC, my parents made the hard decision to let me move away to school. I was definitely needed at home, but consistent with their mantra of "Education was the only way out," they let me go. By letting me go, it meant our family would be down by one farm hand. If you know anything about farming, you know that the loss of one hard working person on a farm will have a greater than one unit impact on overall productivity. This decision was a hard one for them. Years later, two of my sisters would also attend NCSSM; while the remaining siblings would be stellar students in our home county.

NCSSM transformed me from a sponge to an informed consumer of knowledge and later, a producer of knowledge. I learned to synthesize information as a critical thinker. I learned to question, challenge, verify, and counter knowledge claims. Not all knowledge claims are valid for a specific context. Some knowledge claims perpetuate through power and privilege; some emerge through grassroots struggle. Knowledge claims are cultural. After graduating from NCSSM, I attended UNC-Chapel Hill and NC State University. At UNC-Chapel Hill and NC State University, these thoughts carried me through and helped me through many challenges. I worked a few years in industry, as an adjunct instructor, and for the U.S. civil service and county governments. I also married an Army enlisted man and had two kids. We spent a few years living in upstate New York and then southern and central Germany. It dawned on me somewhere along the way that the place where I was happiest and could be most impactful was academia, where knowledge claims are born.

So, after having left for 5 years after my Master of Science degree, I returned to NC State to complete my PhD. I will take a brief step back to my undergraduate years to provide a bit more on context. I changed my major three times during my undergraduate years, starting out as pre-med and then settling on psychology. Still shopping around because I liked EVERY major, yet was required to select only one or two majors, one professor noticed me because I made the highest grade on what seemed to be a pretty tough exam. I was a lively and hardworking student in class, but being the "only" led to a sense of being invisible in class, in spite of my performance. This professor invited me to apply to his summer research program, which focused on using computer programming to design and implement psychological experiments. Not surprisingly, I immediately fell in love with programming, statistical analysis, and the symbolic logic we learned that summer.

The summer research internship led to my senior thesis in psychology. My research professor and one other professor encouraged me to go to graduate school. Exhausted from school, and the energy it took to function as an officer in my sorority, resident hall advisor, and other campus organizations, as well as working at several paid jobs (to cover my own expenses and send money home), I resisted the very idea of graduate school. I even had flashbacks of the days of not eating while an undergraduate student and being too embarrassed to ask anyone for help. I never had a car and would walk several miles per day to and from work, class, and meetings. I actually mastered the art of using multivitamins when the food ran out, until I would get my next paycheck. Note: The mandatory meal plan was not passed until after I graduated from UNC-Chapel Hill, so like many others living in the residence halls, I bought my own groceries and managed to live on about $8 - $10 per week. Plasma donations to earn the $35 for food were starting to get the best of me. I could not take another day of poverty. I needed to go to work. However, the "good" voice in my head kept reminding me of my parents' words – Education is the only way out.

On the third ask by my summer research advisor, I told him I would love to go to graduate school, but had no idea what I wanted to major in, because I still loved every single subject. This is where I learned about industrial engineering. At the time, I knew

I was passionate about social science, design, and technology. This professor looked right at me in the hallway of Davie Hall after class one day. It is still a flashbulb memory for me when he said "You would make a great engineering psychologist." He then described engineering psychology to me, and said I could combine psychology with industrial engineering. He encouraged me to take a look at NC State's Ergonomics program; it was interdisciplinary. And so I did. The program required combining psychology and industrial engineering courses, including a rigorous industrial engineering first year experience seminar that was roughly a crash course for those with no formal industrial engineering background. The psychology was rigorous, with a strong emphasis on systems thinking and quantitative methods, and the faculty were top notch in their fields. They had a strong appreciation for removing disciplinary boundaries. Only an interdisciplinary degree would have attracted me to graduate school, and so I found it at NC State University and enjoyed every minute. To this day, I am only attracted to scholarly environments that are interdisciplinary STEM environments and I consider some of the 43 fields of psychology to be STEM fields. My control of action and environment, otherwise known as my agency, lies in being able to exist at the intersections, not in the silos. My existence at the nexus is fine, albeit challenging. But, I have the right to define it. One of my favorite writers, bell hooks, said it this way:

> *If any female feels she needs anything beyond herself to legitimate and validate her existence, she is already giving away her power to be self-defining, her agency.*
> Bell Hooks

One would think that most scholars at universities think the same way, but as with any tribe, scholarly tribes have traditions, values, rules, and some type of kinship expressed through shared bodies of knowledge; as well as attributes and features of how they approach the craft. Scholars can be biased *toward* those who are like them, and *against* those who are not. Some are extremely biased. I call the extreme ones "academic bigots." They have the sense that their way of thinking or their discipline is superior to others. They act as gatekeepers to block any challenges to the prevailing knowledge claims and approaches. It is believed by some that academic bigots can't possibly pose a real danger if we keep challenging them. Academic bigots might be the most dangerous of all, because they control the flow and dissemination of knowledge. They create legal fictions to serve as constructs or operational definitions in their fields of research, and these legal fictions become principles and practices to use to educate and train other scholars, as well as fund research programs. They also dominate the knowledge claims, which become frameworks to disseminate specific world views. In turn, the bigotry perpetuates inequity, further disenfranchisement, and uneven distribution of benefits from the research we do. Said most powerfully by Cathy O'Neill, who comments in her book, *Weapons of Math Destruction (WMDs)*, on how big data (one of my areas) is being used in an unquestioned way:

> "In this march through a virtual lifetime, we've visited school and college, the courts and the workplace, even the voting booth. Along the way, we've witnessed the destruction caused by WMDs. Promising efficiency and fairness, they distort

higher education, drive up debt, spur mass incarceration, pummel the poor at nearly every juncture, and undermine democracy. It might seem like the logical response is to disarm these weapons, one by one. The problem is that they're feeding on each other." (p. 199)

Don't Apologize and Don't Assimilate

And so it is – working to become the highest rank of professor was, in my opinion, the way to diversify and enhance inclusion of knowledge claims on the globe, and a way to minimize and, ultimately, eliminate the damage caused by biases in STEM and other disciplines. The full professor rank was perceived to be a venue privileged by credibility that would allow me to deconstruct and work toward dismantling the influence of power and privilege in the knowledge claims people make. The rank of full professor brings some level of credibility to one's own claims, but also allows you to raise the issue of the importance of being inclusive across all disciplines. More importantly, achieving the rank of full professor provided opportunities to introduce new frames and perspectives. Scholarly privilege and bias are dangerous to the advancement of knowledge, social justice and equity. Without inclusion at the professorial ranks, we stand to continue to lose out on benefits and outcomes that serve the needs of people of color, women, class minorities, or those otherwise disenfranchised.

So, while the context gave me a clear goal, the mechanisms for achieving that goal were murky. It was made more difficult by my background – low socioeconomic status, first generation college student, African-American, woman, interdisciplinary scholar, and many other things at the nexus. Along came Virginia

Tech's (VT) top-ranked Department of Industrial and Systems Engineering (ISE) where I accepted my first tenure-track faculty position. This department had already placed value on interdisciplinary scholars from an academic standpoint. I was so pleased to get the offer. VT was known for its advances in human factors engineering. One of my most impactful mentors, who really convinced me to go, called it "The Harvard of Human Factors." My mentor's intention was to convey the importance of being at a place known for its interdisciplinary and rigorous human factors and ergonomics research and teaching.

I turned down an industry job in mobile communications that offered $27,000 more in annual salary than the state-based faculty salary offered by VT. But, I went with my passion -- academia. It was at VT that I moved from beginning as an Assistant Professor (1999) to achieving tenure as Associate Professor (2005) and finally achieving the rank of Full Professor (2011). The achieving is not necessarily in the rank, but in the navigation, championing, and change that had to occur along the way. VT is not as diverse as other institutions in terms of underrepresented minorities. This is true across the faculty, staff, and students. It is not for want of discourse and programs to try to increase diversity and inclusion, however. There were many attempts and diversity, especially among underrepresented minorities, increased periodically. But, this was a place where I could go an entire day without seeing anyone else who was African-American, except my family when I came home. My husband and I came to Blacksburg, VA with two kids; we then adopted one more and before adopting, we served as foster parents. It was hard to find African-American families in that area who would do foster care. Like many Black scholars, I believe in being a real part of the Black community and not a scholar in an ivory tower. So, between my husband and I, we coached a girls traveling basketball team that was predominantly African-American, we served as officers in the NAACP (I was a 1.5 term Branch President), and we were active in many other community organizations. Navigating all of these challenges was a real issue because of the sense of isolation and pressure that would consume me at the most inopportune times.

The journey was tough, especially for tenure. There are some things I learned based on experience that are important to share here:

1.   If you don't have an egalitarian spouse or partner, the probability of persisting to the end (full professor) is low.

2.   You cannot forsake your children or other family members in the process of moving toward the professorial ranks. To allow a biased academic system to lead to complete failure in parenting, or sister-ing, cousin-ing, niece-ing, or aunting, is to perpetuate the same institutional and social barriers that often set our children up for failure in this country.

3.   Cross-cultural views of families are different, where majority group members consider family as a more nuclear construct. Family is often much more expansive in other cultures. It is important for university administrators to understand these differences.

4.   You must, above all, maintain a strong sense of identity, cultural, and historical perspective throughout the journey. Always know that context matters as you reason through the activities you need to do to be successful. People will judge you with no knowledge of your context.

5.   Find ways to educate and advance cultural competence.

This includes competence about many aspects of diversity: gender, ethnicity/race, gender identity, sexual identity and orientation, religion, class, geography, etc. Have the courage to begin a dialogue about differences in context, equity, and fairness. If you fail at educating others in your journey or do nothing to enhance cultural competence, then you have not helped others; you have only helped yourself.

6.   Demonstrate inclusive behavior, which includes avoiding forms of privilege such as religious, ethnic, or heterosexual privilege. Find ways to enhance cultural and contextual competence. You may have to manage up (supervisors, administrators, higher-ranked professors), manage sidewise (peers), and manage down (students).

7.   Don't assimilate or surrender your identity or culture.

I was the first African-American Assistant Professor and later tenured professor in that department (male or female). Were it not for the mostly welcoming faculty and staff in that department, I would not have stayed at VT for more than a year. I have learned that a department with an inclusive climate can buffer professors from negative climates at other levels of the university. This mattered tremendously. With the exception of a few, the faculty there were amazing people who really wanted to see more diversity and inclusion among scholars. They were all, well almost all, committed to working extremely hard to make the ISE department a success. Most were very supportive and my two faculty mentors were absolutely effective in making sure I was given the political and inside information about everything that would matter for tenure. With their help, and colleagues in the Black Faculty/Staff Caucus at VT, my trajectory was, for the most part, predictable, but by no means easy. The Department Heads were also very welcoming and inclusive.

I hit the road running. I knew I had to be very good in all three areas of the holy performance trinity --- teaching, research/ scholarship, and service. I call it holy because this way of measuring the value of a scholar is pretty common and people actually accept it as completely valid – when it is only minimally valid for some and completely invalid from a multicultural world view. The problem is that I knew that my gendered and racialized context required me to excel in all three.

In my first semester, I was hit with teaching two courses. I was called before I arrived and the associate department head apologetically explained that, due to a couple of personal challenges faced by a faculty member, my load would have to be two courses rather than the typical one course that new professors were given in their first semester. In the first semester, new professors are given a lighter load so they can build a very strong research enterprise, which means writing proposals and building relationships with other researchers, federal agencies, and relevant industry. In my second year, I flew to Maryland every Monday to teach a course, and flew back that same Monday night to be on the main VT campus on Tuesday morning. I refused to ask for anything special. I did not want my challenges to be any different from any other new professor. I wrote about six extramural proposals in my first year; one of which was funded. One was written and submitted before I even arrived on campus. The next year, I wrote eight proposals, and was PI on most of them. In each year, more proposals were funded, but it was done in collaboration with peers who appreciated my talent, knowledge, and especially, quantitative skills. My teaching was effective as well, but not without the racialized challenges some of the VT students brought forward. But, what they did not know was that I had been an adjunct instructor in some of the toughest places --- maximum security prisons in NY and VA, and military bases with terse Sergeant Majors testing my knowledge and authority. Nothing phased me and I tended to confront and resolve any racialized or genderized behaviors that created a disrespectful environment in the very first week of classes. I also challenged students who thought I should be more of a "Mammy" than a professor. Some assumed I would cut them some slack and assumed that, as a woman and especially a Black woman, that I should be nurturing, lenient, and always open to arguments to negotiate a grade when it was clearly not deserved.

Other things that happened along the way to full professor were appalling to me. For instance, at my mandatory pre-tenure third year review, the Promotion and Tenure Committee (all associate and full professors), questioned my focus and said I needed to have a niche area so I could publish in higher impact, mono-disciplinary journals. I thought my dossier was clear on the knowledge base I was using and the areas of emphasis. The only thing that changed was the application to specific technologies. One of my mentors suggested I go back and find a niche area in my research. To his dismay, I said I would not, but I would, instead, more clearly describe the interdisciplinary knowledge base I was using and how it consistently supported the approaches I used to apply to different technologies. He thought this was a terrible move and would just annoy the committee, who might vote against me because of it. I insisted. I explained to him I was not hired on the basis of being what they wanted me to be and that I was led to believe this department valued interdisciplinary scholars. I was hired on the basis of my scholarly record, which was clearly grounded in interdisciplinary approaches that used the knowledge base of cognition to apply to design and evaluation of systems and technologies. I was not going to compromise. I modified the explanation by making it more clear that I had many application areas, but I did not change the fundamental basis of my interdisciplinary strengths. This worked well, but it also brought out something that I started to repeat to all of my colleagues and the department head. If they did not want what I brought to the table, let me know so I could begin looking for other work.

There were tenured professors who went to lunch on Fridays and untenured professors were strongly encouraged to attend. Many attended. I was never a lunch person, because my husband and I always worked long hours at our jobs. We always had to skip lunch so we could go in two different directions to pick up our kids from day care or after-school programs on time. For instance, I would skip lunch when I worked for the U.S. government in Germany because, by 5 pm, I had to drive full speed from one installation to another, over a mountain and several bridges JUST to get to the daycare center on time. In no way could lunch be a part of my regular workday, unless there was a formal lunch meeting that was relevant to the tasks we were performing. When I arrived at VT and had the same circumstances (well, the mountains but not bridges and driving much more slowly), I was surely not going to change my schedule just to have lunch for political reasons. I went to lunch on a few Fridays here and there, but when I broke it down for professors as to why an every Friday lunch made no sense for my context, they stopped asking. In fact, they would sometimes cheer when I made it to a lunch gathering. I believe their cheers were an acknowledgement that they were at least listening to the diverse life experience I brought to the table (literally and figuratively). I told people more than once that, if our department was so shallow that promotion and tenure were based on these social activities, then tell me now so I could find another place to work.

To this day, I try very hard in my current position to help faculty, students, and staff understand that they are appreciated for who they are and what they bring to the table. They do not have to apologize for differences, but are encouraged to leverage the differences to advance the organization. I also do not apologize for the diversity I bring to the table, and I will not assimilate only to become just like everyone else. This is stated in multiple ways very explicitly. I have also spent a lot of time changing the privileged statements that people make. At first, the winter party was referred to as the "Christmas Party." While not agreed upon by everyone, it was important to change the practice and hope the attitudes would follow. We now have a "Holiday Party" and the decorations are more neutral. Some discussions are totally Afrocentric, and not at all inclusive of the diversity we have in our department. These forms of bias are also addressed. It is important to bring out the issue of bias within predominantly minority groups. We have no more privilege to be biased or bigoted than anyone else. There are some who bring in cultural ideas that are entirely unwelcome, including beliefs that our students are not as smart or talented as we others. I have been at many universities and taught students from all walks of life and from community college to highly-ranked universities. There are NO differences in intellect or talent. The only differences are in the resources these students bring with them and the resources at some of the universities. Resource inequity affects our success, but in the right climate, such as the one I am in now, we have advanced professionals who are able to help under-resourced students achieve and become excellent contributors to society. Very few can claim the same level of expertise in transforming under-resourced students than minority-serving institutions such as NC A&T. Hands down.

Be Real; Be Authentic

My entire tenure stream was spent as authentically as I could be, while also trying very hard to change it from within by navigating personas. I share with others in my organizational unit and across campus that we have to be real. We cannot in any way use legal fictions or false ideas to cover up for the challenges we face, both personally and professionally. I had to confront and overcome my own weaknesses, self-doubt, and downright anger at times. I had to hone my strengths and be open to learning new things. I share these struggles with direct reports because they must know that we are not just a role, but a person who is doing their best to advance success for everyone. In my quest for full professor, without a doubt, I ended up a poster child for all the things that women and minority scholars have warned against. I was overloaded with students. I could fund them, which is one reason. But, secondly, many women and minority students wanted to work with the one African-American woman faculty member. Also, good advisors who care about their students become in high demand, because of word of mouth. Quality of advising, however, decreases with quantity. Now, I explain to many faculty that I see who are experiencing some of the same challenges that they must not fall into this trap. I also deliberately block for professors so they are not over-serviced or over-loaded with students. I repeatedly warn them orally, but also in written form on annual reviews. Balance is crucial to success.

I served on many search committees while advancing to full professor in the department, as well as in the College of Engineering, and university level. I served in offices in the Black Faculty/Staff Caucus and as a Multicultural Fellow. I served in the AdvanceIT program. I advised (co-advised some) to completion 29 ISE doctoral students, 20 ISE master's students, 12 master's projects, over 50 undergraduate projects, and this does not include the informal advising across the university that never made it to my dossier. Every performance letter praised my advising, service, and the many proposals written and funded. I served in my national and international professional societies and on review panels nationwide. I traveled for meetings and invited lectures. I was innovative in my classes. I received a lot of awards. I even consulted on the side (with disclosure to the university) as an expert witness to help support my family. I also quietly helped a lot of women and minority scholars at VT and across the nation by reading and giving feedback on proposals and manuscripts. While my publication numbers were acceptable, I know my publication output suffered due to the high number of students I was advising. The manuscripts that were submitted and accepted were mainly those that were done with my advisees who, of course, needed to take first author. To this day, I still have about 8 of my own first-authored manuscripts sitting on my hard drive, but no time to develop them further. Most of my work related to designing for diverse and inclusive users, so I was at least happy that ideas were getting out there. I had a hard time saying "no" and developed an unhealthy level of John Henryism (or Jane Henryism). Recall the folk story of John Henry, an African American man who drove steel into rock to build a railroad tunnel. A steam-powered hammer was introduced and John Henry was challenged to race against the steam-powered hammer. He won the context, but he died from the stress. So, I became John Henry, racing against the socially constructed barriers that gave advantages to the more privileged. One can go into high gear to overcome these socially constructed barriers, but in the end, the battle could take its toll. I watched others who were under loaded, especially men, enjoy vacations and partners at home who did everything for them. Some practically disappeared during the summer months, while I continued for 12 months every single year and struggled to balance family and work obligations

But, today, I tell faculty that it is not worth it to be a John Henry. I am mastering the art of taking care of myself, so I can be 100% useful to others. In cases of minority-serving institutions, we are often guilty of trying to do more with less, including more work with fewer people. The uneven distribution of funds from our state legislatures, limited endowments, and the relatively lower donations from our alumni make can be challenging. However, we must keep in mind that our faculty, staff, and students have limits as well, and obligations to their families and communities. Work-Life balance really matters. While there is no real way to balance work and life, there are ways to effectively handle the ebb and flow of demands between these two critical components of our lives.

As I look to the mission and vision of NC A&T, I have not lost my commitment to equity in higher education. Every day, I remind myself that none of this was ever about me. I wanted a place that valued the establishment of fair, equitable, inclusive, and culturally competent rules of practice and methods to measure performance. This has not happened anywhere that I am aware of, but, like VT and other universities, we are approaching this ideal at increasing speed. I have hope and optimism, and I carried this forward when I made the difficult decision to leave VT after achieving full professor.

When I found out about the Department Chair position at North Carolina Agricultural and Technical State University (NC A&T), you might be surprised at what I thought at the time. My first thought was the low probability that an engineering department would want a Black woman as chair, regardless of her credentials. Yes, like predominantly White institutions (PWIs), HBCUs struggle with diversity in the ranks and in administration. Some of the same biases exist, and, surprisingly, many of the same Eurocentric ways of thinking about knowledge and knowledge claims are perpetuated by HBCU scholars, some of whom don't strongly question the basis of what they do. This occurs because the only way to get past the knowledge gatekeepers (most of whom are White and male), one has to use majority frameworks and knowledge claims if there is any hope of being published, promoted or having research funded. Deviations lead to declines, and even worse, being shut down by dissemination avenues. It is a vicious cycle. Some have created their own interdisciplinary or multi-culturally valid dissemination venues, but these may suffer from low impact scores and low H-indices because of bias and prevailing privilege among the gatekeepers.

As I deliberated on the NC A&T opportunity, I came to realize that going to this great university would provide a means to continue to challenge the status quo in multiple knowledge domains, and more importantly, to facilitate the success of other faculty, as well as staff and students. I needed to be in this place at this time, because it is the perfect context from which to continue to challenge power and privilege in the research and scholarly arena so the playing field is more fair for faculty and for students; ultimately for society as a whole.

It is interesting that at an HBCU, some of the same diversity and inclusion battles exist. This is interesting but also somewhat disheartening to me. Perhaps it is because, from my world view, I always thought my people were the least prejudiced of all and we were, in fact, closer to the heavens than all others. This is actually a form of racism: the belief that my people are spiritually superior to others. The reality is that we are the same as majority groups and other groups in many ways. We can be prejudiced to the extreme, we can be classist, and many are homophobic and Christian-privileged. It is a sad reality. The difference is that we have not been able to use large political or economic strategies to hurt others with our prejudices; this has remained the domain of majority group members. We need more members of our community with the courage to change things from within and from without.

Courage is an important cognitive act that can lead to significant change. For instance, one day, when I was walking to class, I saw a Muslim woman performing salat in a dirty stairwell on the ground floor while students walked up and down the stairs. This to me was something that needed attention. Students need a place to pray and should have, just like military installations, a place to worship, pray, read, reflect, and do these things regardless of their religion or even if they ascribe to no religion but just need a place to reflect. I began calling around campus to find out if the campus had prayer and reflection spaces. I was told "no". But, here is what makes NC A&T a place that values inclusion and diversity: the request was taken seriously and it sparked more discussion and plans to establish these spaces across campus including inside the library and the new student union. My dean and several other deans took it seriously, and so did our upper administration.

One day, one of our industrial and systems engineering (ISE) graduate students came to my office and asked if she could use the conference room for about 30 minutes because she could not find anywhere else to use her breast pump. She and her husband had worked out a system where they scheduled courses so they could effectively swap the baby in shifts during the day. But, she had to have the baby for longer periods than he because she was breastfeeding. She would rush to find a corner of the research lab or a bathroom stall to feed the baby. They both came up with another plan where she could pump and hand off a bottle to him to ensure they both could balance caring for the baby. The experiment worked in the first week. In the second week, she ran up against a situation where she could not find a private place to pump quickly and get the bottle to him. We did not have lactation stations anywhere on campus. I was a co-principal investigator with the NSF ADVANCE program (institutional transformation) at Virginia Tech. We had lactation stations spread across the VT campus. I was ashamed that I had come to NC A&T and had not once asked where the lactation stations were located. Goodness, I had even received a "Woman of the Year Award" at VT for my advocacy, not only for lactation stations, but for many institutional changes that would level the playing field for women. Yet, I found myself that day staring at our ISE graduate student with an incredulous look on my face that was not directed at her, but directed at my inner self. I had momentarily forgotten the raging battle for gender equity in the academy. You can imagine what happened next, besides of course, reserving the conference room for her and telling her to take her time and use the room any time she wished, if it was available. I called and asked several people, including Human Resources, about lactation stations. There were none to be found. I considered this absence of stations to speak volumes about what we thought of women, students, and families at NC A&T. Obviously, my dean and others took it very seriously and the actions of enhancing inclusion began. I have learned that diversity and inclusion monitoring is a 24 hour activity, because we can easily become comfortable in our privilege and forget that others are not being treated equitably and are struggling in ways we can't even imagine. I am now always mentally scanning for equity and social justice issues and challenges. I cannot turn it off.

In a Chairs' forum one Friday, I raised the question of why chairs were not being given more information regarding the transgender bathroom issue that became highly politicized in North Carolina. Chairs are the ones to prepare their faculty and staff to ensure student diversity and equity for students are always a priority. Yet, the leadership was unusually silent and reserved about the information and the decisions they had made. When I asked the question at the Chairs' forum, you could hear a pin drop. All I could think of at the time was the shaking my head (SMH) emoji. But again, this is what sets NC A&T apart from most other institutions. The effort went forward to open lines of communication regarding transgender students and employees. The communications increased. Our university remained on the right side of history – we had always welcomed transgender students; not that there weren't bigoted students on campus who did not welcome them. But, those students found to disrupt our welcoming climate will face disciplinary action. We had an ingenious work-around to respect their right to use whatever bathroom they wished to use, in spite of NC's intellectually and morally embarrassing policy on bathroom use that was briefly in place for the UNC System.

In addition to this issue, I have, many times, had discussions with my colleagues about the need to acknowledge the complexity of gender and gender identity, including opening their minds to recognize and affirm multiple genders and minimize use of the outdated and incorrect binary classification. I have also expressed openly our support of LGBTQQ (lesbian, gay, bisexual, transgender, queer, questioning) students, faculty, and staff, and asked our administration to take a stand in favor of affirmation.

I don't regret the sacrifices I made, the possible reductions in social capital, nor do I regret the workload I have taken on as a Chair, researcher, teacher, and inclusion and equity advocate. I have also initiated, as part of my executive leadership training, an inclusive research excellence concept in hopes of having the concept disseminated and applied throughout our campus. The goal is to value and conduct research that benefits the broadest range of people in our society, and research that is culturally competent and inclusive. We want to lead in culturally competent, equitable outcomes-based research. We do not wish to perpetuate inequity through research methods, theories, principles, analytical methods, and applied outcomes. As a collective of outstanding intellectuals, NC A&T is poised to address and terminate the atrocities occurring in the research arena today: algorithmic bias, systems that uphold inequality, application of theories that are only valid for majority group members. Inclusive research excellence is about undoing the harm caused by biased research and culturally incompetent researchers who have dominated research and scholarship for the past several centuries. We have a lot to do and HB-

CUs are the best place to do this type of work. It is a great place to be at this time in history!

Inclusive research excellence arose from the opportunity to participate in several intensive leadership development opportunities, including the HERS Institute for Women in Higher Education (Higher Education Recourses), the Center for the Advancement of STEM Leadership (CASL), and the Executive Leadership Program (ELDP) at NC A&T State University. I am thankful to all of them for the growth opportunities, and my CASL coach is an outstanding, accomplished African-American woman who is never afraid to speak out against wrongs. Leadership is about knowing that you are a servant to others and servants have hard jobs that require a keen appreciation of and compassion for every person. Leadership requires a love for knowledge and growth, and the courage to act on that knowledge and speak out when needed. This is what I bring to my HBCU. My Mother told me: Get all the knowledge you can and use it for the greater good. Leadership is also like the mantra my late Father used when he was teaching me to ride my first bike on a very hot day in Fayetteville, NC (Pope Air Force Base). After constantly falling over every time he let go of the bike, the circumstance arose when he let go and I stayed upright. All I heard behind me was an exhausted but very passionate and proud Dad shouting at the top of his lungs, "Keep going. Don't stop. Keep going. Don't stop...."

I still don't rest as much as I should, but I do give priority to taking better care of myself. I would have liked to have a comfortable and pressure free life, but that is not my purpose here. My purpose is now to help others achieve success and to work toward scholarly justice and equity. This walk is an existential one that will take courage, selflessness, and fortitude.

And so it is, we are all at a nexus that is a whirlwind of change. We must embrace this fact of reality in our minority serving institutions. To all of my colleagues of color, especially my Sista colleagues, in the scholarly struggle in the great halls of academia: Get and own the knowledge, embrace growth, have courage to speak out, be encouraged at all times, and above all, keep going, don't stop!

References

Heller, M. (1988). *Code switching: Anthropological and Sociolinguistic Perspectives.* Berlin: Muyton de Gruyter.

Molinsky, A. (2007). Cross-cultural code-switching: The psychological challenges of adapting behavior in foreign cultural interactions. *Academy of Management Review, 32,* 622-640.

O'Neill, C. (2016). *Weapons of Math Destruction: How Big Data Increases Inequality and Threatens Democracy.* New York: Broadway Books.

PART II

PATH TO SENIOR LEADERSHIP POSITIONS

CHAPTER 8

Keep Your Eyes on the Prize

Cheryl A. Swanier, PhD, EdD

Your past shapes your present;
it is the foundation of your future.
Sandra K. Johnson

My life story has authentically informed my leadership abilities and my trajectory to a senior leadership position as department chair has not been without challenges. I never once thought that through all of the opposition that I have endured during my lifetime would provide me the opportunity to transform lives and impact communities. "The journey to authentic leadership begins with understanding the story of your life. Your life story provides the context for your experiences, and through it, you can find the inspiration to make an impact in the world," (George et al, 2007). Truly, I have inspired many students and faculty to fulfil their chosen vocation by being my authentic self. It is through storytelling that I share the impact that I have made at minority serving institutions. But, I must first sketch the context by acknowledging some of the many structures that shaped and formed the leader that I have become.

The Context

I have always aspired to become a leader since my childhood. I often participated in organizations such as 4-H, Future Homemakers of America, Future Business Leaders of America, Brooks County

High School Marching Band and other organizations. These organizations were key players in the formation of my leadership skills and abilities. My church Bethel African Methodist Episcopal (AME) Church also played a critical role during my formative years in developing me as a young leader. I was given leadership responsibility as a child. I taught Sunday school, played the piano for both Sunday school and Sunday morning church services. I served on the Junior Usher Board and sung in the Junior Choir. Often times, I had to review the Sunday school lesson and teach even my peers about the Bible. I also had to count money from the Sunday school offerings that were collected. I served as Secretary of the Sunday school. I was given so many opportunities to develop and demonstrate leadership skills with no formal training. Soon I became entrepreneurial as I started a singing group along with my elder sister called the *Celestial Angels*. I played the piano while my sister directed the choir. We went from church to church singing praises.

During my senior year in high school, my peers elected me as the Senior Class President and I was also first runner up to Miss Brooks County High School. In addition, I served as the Co-Captain and Choreographer of the marching band flag team. My dream of becoming a senior leader did not stop there. After graduating from Albany State and attending the Ohio State University, I always aspired to become a Chief Executive Officer (CEO) of a major corporation. While working for IBM in upstate New York, it was my career goal to be a CEO. This aspiration quickly diminished once I reached a glass ceiling like many minority women in Corporate America. I lost hope and moved back to Georgia and worked as a senior programmer. While I continued working in computing, I also began to pursue a doctorate in higher education administration at Auburn University. I constantly dreamed of the presidency as I completed my doctorate.

Eventually, I reinvented myself and became a classroom teacher. I became a Mathematics Department Chair and lead several efforts to change the attitudes towards math by both students and teachers through various educational programming such as Math Night. This event made mathematics fun and engaging as we played various mathematical games, fellowshipped and ate pizza. These type of educational events and other mathematical activities favorably increased interest in math and student achievement in mathematics increased. I began to blossom as a leader in both middle school and high school mathematics. I had a passion for teaching and learning. I knew how to strategically get students to like math and increase math scores. However, I still kept wondering how I was going to be a college president working in a high school on the south side of town with at-risk students. The idea of becoming a college president continued to plague me.

I had taken leadership classes at Auburn University and decided that I wanted to become a president of a Historically Black College and University (HBCU). After being a high school math teacher for almost seven years, it was time to reinvent myself again. The idea of being a HBCU president was still weighing heavily on my mind and seemed so far in the distance. No matter what, I could not shake the idea of becoming a college president.

After attending a social function between rival institutions, I met a childhood friend who was a provost at an HBCU. I was totally appalled that he had attained such great success in higher education. I thought to myself, "If he is a Provost, I should be a President." I quickly discerned that my dream of being a college president was not just a far-fetched idea, but it could be achieved.

After much conversation with my friend, he asked me to send him my resume. Within two weeks, I had submitted my application, interviewed for a Department Chair position, and accepted a position as an Associate Professor of Computer Science. Now I was on the path to realizing my full potential.

The Academy

Once I began teaching computer science at the college level, I hit the ground running. There was no computing organization for computer science students. The students had not conducted any undergraduate research nor had they been exposed to presenting research at conferences. I re-established a student chapter of the Association of Computing Machinery (ACM) where there were only three members. We took our first flight to Microsoft Research in Redmond, Washington to a computing conference. One of my students had never flown before in an airplane. This gave me an opportunity to expose my students to computing at the corporate level in another region of the country. We started attending conferences such as Grace Hopper and TAPIA. My students and I were traveling all across the country presenting research. My colleagues began to say that I was trying to outshine them. I was not. I was in my element. My leadership skills were in full effect. I was on my way to fulfilling my lifelong dream. I was making a positive impact as a woman of color at this minority serving institution. Both my corporate experience and my K-12 experience played a critical role in my career advancement in the academy.

Leaders at the minority serving institution began to notice my efforts and commitment to the students. I was serving on committees and chairing university committees. I was asked to serve on search committees. Soon I became nationally known. President Obama selected me as a Champion of Change for Technology Inclusion. Next, Ebony Magazine recognized me as a Power 100, that is, one of the 100 most influential African Americans in my discipline. National organizations such National Center for Women in Technology recognized my mentoring of undergraduate students in research. I was receiving one award after another. All of a sudden, there was a shift in status. I got tenure within four years of being at the university. I was only one step away from being a full professor. Three years prior, I was on the south side of town teaching mathematics to students who were labelled 'at-risk.' My life suddenly shifted upward to the point it was almost scary. So many positive things were occurring.

After serving eight years at a minority serving institution, I accepted a leadership position as a Department Chair of Mathematics and Computer Science and was named an Endowed Professor at another minority serving institution in a different state. I knew as a leader that my faculty was looking to me to bring about a positive change within the department. The Department of Mathematics and Computer Science did not have ABET accreditation, which is an international accreditation agency. I was tasked to lead this effort. With no prior experience with accreditation, I immediately started having weekly meetings with the computer science faculty. Within in two months, we submitted our initial preliminary self-study report. A year later, we had our initial site visit with the ABET Team. We were successful in receiving no deficiencies. This almost did not make sense. How is it that this woman of color enters into this minority serving institution and leads such an effort with all the cards stacked against her and receives no deficiencies? This is almost unheard of. There was only three computer science faculty when I arrived. By the time the final ABET report was submitted, there were six full-time computer science faculty. Simply amazing!

Leadership means making a difference, having a positive impact, and empowering people. In order to make a difference, one has to be ready, willing, and able to get into the trenches and get their hands dirty. Leadership is hard work. One has to sometimes go where others will never go. Leadership involves taking risks and doing things that others may not ever have the courage to do. Leaders are visionary. Without a vision, the people that you serve will perish. As a leader, one has to be willing to serve others. It is imperative that a leader has a servant's heart. Leadership is not about do what I say, but what can I do for you. Hard work, passion, and dedication to mission and the vision of the institution play a vital role in making a difference at a minority serving institution.

What does authentic leadership mean for me? Authentic leadership means being true to you, not being anyone else. Authentic leadership means, "not faking it to make it." Others can see through fakeness. "For authentic leaders, there are special rewards. No individual achievement can equal the pleasure of leading a group of people to achieve a worthy goal. When you cross the finish line together, all the pain and suffering you may have experienced quickly vanishes. It is replaced by a deep inner satisfaction that you have empowered others and thus made the world a better place. That's the challenge and the fulfilment of authentic leadership" (George et al, 2007). When I reflect upon the impact that I have made on both students and faculty lives and the differences that I made in the lives of others, I get a feeling like no other that I have changed their world while remaining true to myself. For those students and faculty that I have positively impacted, I am in constant communication with them. My leadership was not in vain. Because I have helped someone, my living and my leadership have not been in vain.

References

George B., Sims P., McLean A. N., Mayer D. (2007). Discovering your authenticleadership. *Harvard Business Review*, 85(2-8).

CHAPTER 9

The Impact of Silent Service
Kimarie Engerman, PhD

The Journey

On the eve of submitting my contribution to *Women Called to Lead*, I was appointed Interim Dean of the College of Liberal Arts and Social Sciences (CLASS). It was sudden and completely un-expected. My predecessor at that time was with the university for over 30 years and was leaving to join the newly elected governor's administration team for our Territory. Now the funny thing with that situation was that I found out the Dean was leaving while listening to the governor's press conference. I was only listening because a family member was being appointed to a senior staff position. So, I was totally shocked and caught-off guard when I heard my Dean's name mentioned as part of the governor's senior staff. That moment is now embedded in my flashbulb memory.

The press conference then led to a whirlwind of events. As the chatter of who the new Interim Dean was going to be travelled throughout my college, and even the university, it did not dawn on me that I would be considered as a potential "option" for the appointment as Dean. I purposely used the word "option" because I did not express an initial interest in the position. Two months prior to the press conference, I had participated in the commence-ment ceremony at the Chicago School of Professional Psychology for receiving a Post-Graduate Certificate in Academic Leadership as part of the National Science Foundation funded Opportunities for UnderRepresented Scholars (OURS) Program. The title of *academic leader* was still new to me and I was still learning to embrace that identity.

Additionally, towards the end of the OURS Program, although I was not fully certain of my ultimate goal, I drafted what I thought was my academic leadership pathway. This was comprised of seven steps:

Step 1: Obtain additional leadership experiences at my institution

Step 2: Participate in a Faculty/Administrator Exchange Program at another institution

Step 3: Obtain the rank of Full Professor

Step 4: Become the Chair of my department

Step 5: Become the Dean of my college

Step 6: Become the Provost at my institution

Step 7: Become President of my institution

At the time, for me, Step 7 was really thinking of the impossible and a position beyond my wildest imagination. Although I was laughing when I created my pathway, I figured I might as well aim as high as I could possibly go in academia. In life, dreams do become a reality. I decided to dream big, set a high goal, and see where the chips fall. Do I really want to be President? I did not know. Besides, some days I closely observed the Provost and wondered how she does it all especially when she has to fight with the faculty for things that make logical sense. Right now, I know I do not have that temperament. This is definitely a good thing because I still have more developing and growth to do as an academic leader. Furthermore, I am not in a rush to get to the top.

Anyway, in reviewing my steps, one can easily see that the

dean's position was completely off my immediate radar. I figured the Interim Dean would logically be one of the five Chairs who were all at the institution for a number of years. It was obvious that some of them indeed wanted the position. This of course led to some resentment when I was appointed which would be expected.

At the time, I was a Provost Fellow. In one of my regularly scheduled meetings with the Provost, she shared the process in regards to selecting the Interim Dean. It involved meeting individually with members of the former dean's administrative team which comprised of Chairs and Directors. She also mentioned another option she was considering was to appoint me. Appoint me? How did I get added to the pool of potential candidates? I was blown away. According to her, completing the OURS Program made me qualified. It was ideal because I had the training needed.

The whole thing felt surreal. One moment I found out my Dean was leaving and in the next moment I am the replacement. Letting my nerves get the best of me, I agreed to accept the position with the understanding that a search will be conducted immediately. Everything happened so suddenly that I did not have time to mentally prepare myself. Unlike *Esther in the Bible*, I recognized it was not my time to fully accept the position. I told my colleagues I was not applying for the position and remained true to my word. I think I did that to ease the bruise they got to their egos. They had a right to feel insulted. They were the known leaders in the college. I kept an extremely low profile. I sat in the last row at college meetings; although I was fully cognizant of what was happening, I never participated in the pointless squabbles that occurred. The extent of my participation was to announce the dates for Psi Chi, The International Honor Society induction ceremony, UVI Research Day, and Academic Awards Ceremony.

From the outside looking in, I could not be the person chosen to lead. The resentment created by my appointment was obvious when I convened my first meeting and only two out of six of the invited Chairs attended. Nevertheless, about seven weeks into my appointment, my biggest critic became my number one supporter. After a college meeting, the individual told me directly about the initial concerns with my selection, but now seeing me in action and interacting with me over the past few weeks made it clear why the Provost selected me. The person further added that I was the best person for the position.

You see, the Provost knew what my colleagues were oblivious to knowing. They were so busy focusing on the individuals in the front of the room who talked a good talk, but produced nothing, that they missed the impact I was silently making along the way. I am a covert leader; this makes it easily for me to be overlooked. According to Mintzberg (1998), covert leaders are those work together on a project or task with a group of highly qualified individuals. I lead from within.

Over the years, I was busy serving my institution without giving any thought to the impact I was making. I was driven to improve my institution and make it a better place. I led initiatives. I worked collegially with others and did what was needed to ensure the university's needs were met. My work ethic, commitment to tasks, attention to detail, and genuine interest in what I was doing allowed me to be successful. The Provost knew this first-hand from the outcomes of initiatives I led that had a university-wide impact.

Institutional Impact

When I pause to reflect on the impact I have made to the institution, three initiatives come readily to mind: (1) academic advising; (2) faculty scholarly development; and (3) faculty mentoring program.

Academic Advising

The first initiative was my Action Learning Project (ALP) completed as part of the OURS Program. The ALP was on academic advising. The topic was selected because of findings from the National Science Foundation, Education Research Project (ERP) in which I served as Principal Investigator. In this longitudinal study, students were consistently dissatisfied with the university's advising services. I found that to be rather problematic because the university's policy required students receive pin from their academic advisor in order to register for classes. Implicit in this policy was that faculty were going to provide academic services prior to giving the pin to students. This clearly could not be the case if students were dissatisfied. For my ALP, I surveyed students and faculty as well as documented best practices at our Peer and Aspirational Peer Institutions. Based on my findings, I created recommendations on how advising could be improved. I met with the Provost and President individually to share the results of my ALP.

My ALP impacted the institution. Academic Advising was the theme for the end of the semester Faculty Institute. The Faculty Institute is mandatory for all full-time faculty and is held after final exams and before commencement. Recognizing the importance of this topic, the President was present to provide opening remarks. The Provost was also present to speak on academic advising. I was responsible for organizing the agenda. My ALP was presented and the remainder of the day was comprised of topics related to academic advising. A few faculty identified as model advisors shared their advising techniques. The Faculty Institute sparked an interest in academic advising and it became a hot topic on campus. The following year it was requested to be the topic again at the next Faculty Institute.

The work I did on academic advising had an additional institutional impact. Improving academic advising became one of the Provost's goals the following academic year. I became Chair of the newly convened Academic Advising Committee. The outcome was the creation of the university wide academic advising plan. Using recommendations in the plan, the university implemented an electronic advising system. Now when advising is discussed, my name and the work I did are frequently mentioned.

Faculty Scholarly Development

Another institutional impact was the Faculty Development Writing Group (FDWG) that I started. During the reception for one of the OURS's residency, Stephanie Luster-Teasley and I were talking about our scholarly productivity. I shared with Stephanie my need to increase my publications. Stephanie recommended I use a journal writing book she used with her students. I ran with Stephanie's recommendation and immediately ordered the book. Once I got the book, I realized I needed a network to support me through the process and hold me accountable. I invited two colleagues I knew also needed to obtain publications. One was a new junior faculty and the other was a research faculty. We were productive that semester and had a few accomplishments.

My writing group was occurring during the time I was

serving as a Provost Fellow. In meeting with the Provost bi-weekly, I would often share with her our accomplishments. Recognizing the benefits and seeing the success of the group on a small level, the Provost asked if I could implement it university-wide to junior faculty. The group became officially known as the FDWG. The FDWG now serves as a university-wide support system to help faculty increase their scholarly productivity. At the start of each semester members submit specific writing goals. Then at the end of the semester, I conduct an evaluation to find out if goals were accomplished and how participating in the group helped accomplish goals.

The FDWG meets weekly and I serve as the facilitator. Some outputs of the group are journal publications, grants, conference abstract submissions, conference presentations, and book chapters. One success story that readily comes to mind is a tenure-track faculty who had no research agenda when the individual joined the group. The individual had no publications and not even an identified topic. Had the individual continued on that path, obtaining tenure would not have been possible. Participating in the group resulted in the individual developing multiple research projects, and publishing many journal articles and book chapters. The individual received tenure and the individual's accomplishment spoke to the value of the FDWG.

By design, the FDWG was one of the best kept secrets at the university. I find when things are too large, people bring drama and create chaos. Therefore, at the beginning of the semester, I would invite all new junior faculty to join the group. Unfortunately, not all would accept the invitation. Now due to the tremendous impact the FDWG has made on faculty's scholarly productivity, it has received a lot of publicity. Some of the same individuals who initially declined the invitation are now asking to join. Also, some departments are seeking ways to implement various forms of the FDWG. The FDWG is frequently highlighted in the President's report to the Board of Trustees.

Faculty Mentoring Program

As a Provost Fellow, I was interested in planning and implementing a Junior Faculty Mentoring Program. This interest was sparked by my experiences as a junior faculty. During my early years, the Administrative Assistant for the department served as my mentor. She took me under her wings and provided me with critical information. My colleagues were collegial, but no one took the time to inform me of various "unwritten" policies at the university, how things were to be done, mandatory activities, and just regular day-to-day stuff. Ms. D saw to it that I was in the know. She shared with me opportunities at the university and told me to keep a copy of everything I did because I would need the information for my Record of Activities at the end of the year. Doing so was easy for me because while in graduate school, I had to do my advisor's annual report. It was such a daunting task because my advisor was a director of a research center in addition to being a full professor and had lots of activities to report each year. Now as a junior faculty, I was glad for those experiences because it made doing my Record of Activities extremely easy.

Ms. D also made sure I kept my eyes opened and remained alert to my surroundings. This was mainly for my personal protection. Without mentioning any names, she told me to be careful when I went to a certain area in the building because some individuals were known not to keep their hands to themselves. That information kept me guarded. Years later, I indirectly experienced exactly what Ms. D was telling me. It was a total shock to me because it was not the individual I physically distanced myself from all those years. I reminded myself in that moment to not judge the book by its cover.

Throughout the years, I shared the information I obtained from Ms. D, both professionally and personally, with new faculty. I do believe my success at the institution is credited to Ms. D and a mentor I eventually sought outside of my college. The mentor provided me with opportunities for advancement. Recognizing not all junior faculty are fortunate as I was, I created the Junior Faculty Mentoring Program (JDMP) as one of my Provost Fellow's task.

To create the JFMP, I surveyed individuals identified by the Office of the Provost as junior faculty. I asked about their mentoring experiences and recommendation for such a program. Also, I reviewed best practices in junior faculty mentoring at UVI's Peer and Aspirational Peer Institutions. Based on the findings from my survey and insight from the other institutions, I developed a faculty mentoring model that was best suited for my institution. Guidelines for the program were created along with mentee profile form, mentor profile form, and a confidentiality agreement. The program description was shared with the entire faculty for review and feedback before its implementation.

The JFMP was implemented university-wide. As recommended by the survey participants, it is rather informal in that the mentor and mentee determines the nature of the relationship and frequency of meetings. I serve as Program Coordinator. Mentees are allowed to select their mentors who do not necessarily have to be in their department or college. If a mentee cannot find a mentor, I will identify one for him or her. Throughout the semester,

I do periodic check-ins with mentees to see how things are progressing. I intervene with mentors when needed.

The program is growing. Nevertheless, it has had a few challenges along the way particularly with mentors doing their part. Some mentors have done an outstanding job and have gone way beyond what was asked of them. This includes doing classroom observations to provide the junior faculty with pedagogical advice. A few have not followed-up with their mentee outside of agreeing to serve as mentor. Although the survey recommendation was to keep it informal, I plan to impose a little more structure.

Mentoring is close to my heart and is something I do naturally. I was honored when my students presented me with an *Outstanding Mentor Award.* As I was with students in the past, my overall intent is to make the JFMP one of the best initiatives for faculty on campus. I recently completed a National Mentor Facilitator Training and will be using that information to improve the JFMP.

A goal for the VI EPSCoR grant from the National Science Foundation is to establish a university mentoring plan and program. Because of the work I am doing with the JFMP, I was asked to serve on the institution's Mentoring Steering Committee. The university is committed to mentoring. I will continue to be the voice for faculty, and of course students.

Back on Track

I served as Interim Dean for one full year. The search was completed five months into my term; that was the quickest search I had ever seen at my institution. Staying true to my word, I did not apply for the position. The candidate selected could not start until the following Spring semester. Therefore, I served in the position for two semesters. It was truly an experience.

The first semester was extremely hard. I would go to sleep at night with my heart racing thinking of all the emails I failed to respond to during the day and night. Many nights I silently cursed the person who invented email. A colleague told me my problem was caused by me being too responsive to people. I needed to let them figure things out and stop helping with each issue.

During that same first semester, two things happened around the same time that tremendously impacted me professionally: (1) my Psychology colleague died; and (2) going to South Africa with the OURS Program to present my ALP. Losing a colleague is painful in itself. Then having to deal with it from an administrative side added a different dynamic. *What was the university's policy on disclosing such information to the community?* There was no policy! Now mind you, I found out my colleague passed away by just happening to be skimming through the Saturday newspaper. It took me a minute to even realize what I was seeing. Here it was this familiar, friendly face was staring at me. I know it sounds silly now, but I turned and asked my sister for validation. I asked if it was really the obituary and if I was reading the name correctly. I knew my colleague was ill, but how could she die and I find out in the obituary.

Her death led to a spiral of events. Some people felt I handled it wrong. But again, what was the university's policy on disclosing such information to the community? *Silence.* After composing myself after reading the obituary, I immediately sent a notice to the President and Provost. I then sent a notice to the entire college. I waited. I recalled on many occasions receiving notification that an employee passed away. This time nothing was disseminated to the entire university. It turned out that there was no policy. I told those close to the deceased that they had my full support in planning a memorial service. Nothing happened.

Within a few short weeks, I went to Cape Town, South Africa with the OURS Program. My ALP was selected as one of four to be presented at the Gender Summit. Only God knew how much I needed that getaway. I used that time away to clear my mind, do some soul searching, and just do some sisterly bonding with my OURS Sisters. As women in the academy, we are sometimes so alone and in need of that sisterly connection. It felt good to be with my sisters and receive support as I unloaded some of the challenges I was facing as an academic leader.

Well, while in Cape Town another colleague died. This individual was from a different college, was popular, and had an outgoing personality. The university was preparing to send an announcement to the university community about her sudden passing. I received an email asking for information about my Psychology colleague/faculty to include in the announcement. Interesting. For close to three weeks nothing was said about my faculty. Now all of sudden there was an urgency to obtain information.

Those chain of events forced me to really evaluate my value and worth to the institution. I wondered what would happen if I died today. Would the institution take the time to send an announcement? Would my passing go unnoticed? I was working so hard. Yet, in the grand scheme of things there was a possibility that although my work impacted the institution, me as an individual, meant nothing to the institution.

I changed. I remained responsive, but adopted the attitude that tomorrow is another day and it was okay not to complete all the tasks on my list. Also, I started being mentally and not only physically present with my family. Usually I would be physically with family, but mentally engaged with my laptop. That was no longer the case. I know it may sound strange, but I am thankful for my colleague dying when she did at that point in my career as an academic leader. Anyway, I eventually sent the notice to the entire community and organized a remembrance for her on campus that was reflective of her personality.

The second semester as Interim Dean was not as difficult as the first. I understood what needed to be done. As can be expected, there were still stressors along the way, but things fell into place. I had established a good relationship with my faculty; morale was high. I accomplished the goals the Provost tasked me with when I was appointed. Overall, I ended my term on a positive note. I was tired and off to sabbatical I went.

Back at It

As I write this submission, I am now Acting Dean of my college. The Dean who served after my term as Interim Dean resigned. Her resignation, after serving three semesters, came as a surprise. A few hours prior to learning of her resignation, an announcement was made that I was appointed director of a center on campus. I reluctantly accepted the director position to help out. I still had the belief that I needed to be a Full Professor before I accepted any permanent academic leadership position.

In the middle of transitioning to the director position, I was asked to serve this time as Acting Dean. Morale in the college was extremely low. Someone was needed to bring the college together. I was the best person for the position. My specified conditions were met and I accepted the offer. The college warmly received my return.

I have learned that everything happens for a reason. More importantly, timing is everything. In life people will not fully appreciate what they have until they experience something else that is unpleasant. I will continue on my academic leadership pathway and see what the future unfolds. You never know, I might really be president one day.

Reference

Mintzberg, H. (1998) Covert leadership: Notes on managing professionals. *Harvard Business Review*, 140-147.

CHAPTER 10

Charting Your Own Course

Farrah Ward, PhD

Early Leadership Training – School

Growing up I was blessed to have a mother and father who truly believed in me and inspired me to be successful. I always say that my parents never pressured me to do anything but always encouraged me to do everything. I did everything from being a member of the Odyssey of the Mind team and Junior Civitan to playing varsity volleyball. In elementary school I was a head safety patrol officer and served as Student Government President in the 8th and 12th grade. I participated in several local and statewide leadership programs and remember using Robert's Rules of Order for several years in high school. I always felt comfortable giving presentations and remember speaking in front of large crowds very early in my teens. Growing up I was very outgoing and remember taking the Myers-Briggs personality test and finding out I was an ESFP and thinking well that makes a lot of sense. First, yes I remember my Myers-Briggs score from 11th grade, you'll hear about my self-awareness later on, and second yes I was a spontaneous performer with common sense and a helping hand. In school I sometimes felt that I was a "stereotypical contradiction", I graduated second in my class but was also voted most popular, a combination that on the surface may not seem to go together but for me it worked. As an undergraduate I attended North Carolina A&T State University (NC A&T), an HBCU, where I received solid mentoring and grooming. I continued participating in leadership activities and served as Speaker Pro-Temp of the Student Senate and later parliamentarian for my sorority. When I went to graduate school at North Carolina State University (NCSU) it was a completely different environment than NC A&T; students at NCSU where highly competitive, the males drastically outnumbered the females, and I became the only minority in the vast majority of my courses. Although I made friends during graduate school it was definitely during this time that I became a little more introverted and started to really take time to think more about my purpose. When I think back about what motivated me to get involved in so many leadership experiences throughout grade school and undergraduate, I am convinced that I believed I could make a difference. Although I can't pinpoint what drove me to seek out each leadership position that I held, I do know that I was never a driven by a need for prestige or power. I always sought to use my position to do what was best for others and even though I enjoyed being the life of the party I never enjoyed being recognized for my accolades or achievements. On the surface my early leadership training may suggest that my rise in higher education was quite deliberate; however, the reality is that the thought of entering into higher education administration never even crossed my mind and my path was a bit windy.

The Beginning of My Career

When I first went on the job market I remember my Ph.D. advisor asking me how many schools I planned on applying to, me responding 10, and him laughing hysterically and saying try more like 100. I believe we settled on 60 but needless to say I was very confused about the higher education hiring process and quickly realized it was much different than what I imagined. I was fortunate to receive several interviews from a variety of universities which was a wonderful accomplishment. While interviewing for one job I remember being challenged rather aggressively on the validity of one of my research findings. Since I had been buried in my research for several years I was quite confident that I was correct and that the gentleman challenging me was incorrect. During the interview we went back and forth about the results and I remember saying "I respectfully agree to disagree". Throughout my years in higher education I have encountered events like this more times than I wish to admit but I am happy to know that this pivotal event prepared me for the future. So no matter how much you know there will always be someone who wants to challenge you, make sure that your information is backed by facts, defend your position, but agree to disagree when needed.

I was lucky enough to secure my "dream job" right out of graduate school. A tenure-track position at a state school with a 3-3 teaching load, realistic research expectations for tenure, and just an hour away from my Ph.D. advisor. There were three other African-Americans in the department when I joined, one other Math Ph.D. and two mathematics education professors with doctorates from well-respected schools, something I had not encountered at any majority institution that I had previously visited. The initial months at my new job were wonderful but as time went on it was clear that there were political agendas going on within the department that I did not notice during the interview process. As time went on the politics became more pronounced and I started disliking my work environment. I found myself spending more time having pre-meetings with faculty before department meetings to discuss possible vote outcomes on agenda items and less time mentoring students. Although later on in my career I would understand how invaluable discussing agenda items with faculty before a big vote was, this was not how I wanted to spend my time as a junior faculty. The thought of switching institutions after only two years of teaching was quite scary and numerous thoughts went through my mind; what would I say when they asked why I was leaving, was this political jockeying just a natural part of higher education, what if I can't find a job. In the end I decided to take the risk and went on to find my real dream job. Although I could have been bitter about having to relocate for another job, what I realized was that even when things don't turn out the way you want them to there is always something to learn, take those jewels and try not to repeat the same mistake.

At my new institution, a state HBCU, I was blessed to be offered a leadership position within the first year of being hired. I served as an Assistant Director of a Center and ran a summer internship program for undergraduate mathematics students. After only a few months at my new institution I began to realize that I was serving on numerous committees and my research time was quickly getting eaten up by meetings. My advisor had always stressed the importance of being active with my research but the distance from my advisor, lack of collaborators, and dwindling free time made it hard for me to continue with my initial research agenda. It was at that instance that I looked within the department to see what was missing and how I could contribute to its success. One area where the department was growing but lacked faculty resources was mathematics education. Although my M.S. and Ph.D. are both in mathematics, my B.S. is in mathematics education and I had published a few articles on training student teachers. Once I decided to focus on mathematics education I actively looked for ways I could enhance the department's mathematics education program. Realizing that the M.S. in mathematics education was not authorized to issue advanced licenses I wrote the report to receive approval from the North Carolina Department of Public Instruction to issue advanced licenses for the M.S. program. I also received a National Science Foundation grant for $667,000 to give scholarships to mathematics education majors. It was during this pivotal time that I understood how identifying key voids and developing a plan to address those issues could truly transform a program.

When I first entered academia my sole focus was on becoming the best professor I could be and I never thought of becoming an administrator. When I was appointed as Chair of the Department of Mathematics and Computer Science it was a complete surprise. I initially questioned why I was chosen as Chair since I had no experience as an administrator, was the youngest member in my department, and had not sought out the position. I was unsure how my colleagues would react to me being their supervisor and I knew that it was important that I developed strategies for working with both colleagues and students. I had never considered what I wanted to accomplish as a department chair and while I would like to say I spent countless nights researching characteristics of successful chairs, the truth is it was trial by fire. It only took me about one month to realize that the role of department chair was one of the most difficult positions on campus and required a constant shifting of roles. On most days I operated as a front-line manager, dealing with day-to-day issues as they arose and making sure that the department ran smoothly. On other days I played the role of advocate, working with upper administration on behalf of my students and faculty to ensure that they received the resources they needed to be successful. Department Chairs serve as a front line of defense and are close enough to the ground that they understand how: scheduling a course one hour earlier can affect an individual who is working a full-time job, students' complaints can vary in their level of truth, and changing one sentence in a policy can affect enrollment and retention numbers. On the other hand, as a department chair you are often requested to serve on several committees which allow you to understand the complexities involved in running Academic Affairs and the inner workings of the university. While I know several successful administrators who never served as department chair or dean, the information I gained while serving as chair for 6 ½ years provided me with information and tools that I use every day in my current role as Associate Vice Chancellor for Academic Affairs. As you move along the leadership path it is important not to rush to get to the next level, learn as much as you can at each stage and save it for when you advance in your career.

Learning to Lead

While serving as department chair I was invited by my dean to apply for the Opportunities for Underrepresented Scholars (OURS) Post-Graduate Certificate in Academic Leadership program. My participation in OURS was the single most pivotal moment in my leadership journey. Prior to my participation in OURS my department had experienced some success. We developed a detailed annual evaluation instrument, had the highest retention rate at the university, and ranked #1 in the nation for graduating the largest number of African Americans with a M.S. in mathematics for two consecutive years. While I knew that the department had made great strides from where we were when I became department chair I knew we were far from reaching our full potential.

I initially thought that our stagnation was primarily because of the lack of desire and commitment from the faculty but what the OURS program taught me was that as a leader I played a key part in my department's success and failure. Below are what I believe are three of the most essential components of being an effective leader.

Self-Awareness

Being self-aware is a critical component of being an effective leader. Understanding one's strengths and weaknesses allows one to be honest with themselves without being "overly critical or unrealistically hopeful" (Goleman, 1998, p.85). A few years ago I decided to retake that Myers-Brigg exam that I first took as an 11th grader. Feeling like I became an introvert during graduate school I wondered if Myers-Brigg would confirm my suspicion. When I first took the exam and read the results I knew something was not right because the person they were describing was not me at all so I took it again and made sure I was being honest. As soon as I finished I got my new results, ISTJ-A, the introverted organized logician that follows the rules and standards, yep that was me. Being self-aware means that I am open to receiving critique and am always thinking about how I can grow from others' comments. During my first year as chair I couldn't wait to get the feedback from my faculty and focus on how I could make improvements in my new role as chair. As someone who is self-aware I am rarely surprised during my end of year evaluations because I usually have done a self-assessment of where I can improve and am eager to hear what my supervisor has to add (Goleman, 1998). I often tell people that I am an implementer. I am organized and structured in my thinking and when given a project logically think through each step of the process in my head. Although I sometimes have good ideas I do not consider myself a visionary so I often talk with others about their ideas on how we can improve different areas. In leadership it is important to know your strengths and weaknesses and not to be confused by the two.

Humility

As a leader I have learned that it is more important to get the job done and make sure your employees are recognized for their effort than to receive individual praise. Faculty members do not respond to a leader who wants all of the credit and will quickly shut down if they perceive that all of your ideas are intended for individual praise. On the other hand, faculty members who are praised and rewarded for their effort will oftentimes work harder to achieve the goal. During my second year as department chair I felt that sometimes when I had an idea about what the department should do certain faculty would immediately find a reason why this should not be done; however, I quickly realized that it was not the idea itself that was being rejected but the fact that it was perceived as a top down mandate. Instead of being upset about faculty rejecting an idea because it was mine I began discussing my ideas with faculty before the meeting, a skill I learned at my first job, and had them bring it up during meetings which most of the time resulted in a positive outcome. As a leader you must realize when it is more important to get the job done than to receive individual credit for the goal being accomplished.

Integrity

As a leader it is essential to display integrity in every situation. Integrity and honesty are two of the key characteristics that are at the core of who I am but are occasionally challenged as a leader. Being a leader means that you are often privy to confidential information which cannot be disclosed so you are constantly challenged with balancing one's integrity with your professional job as an administrator. As a leader I try to be open and honest about decisions that are being made as long as they do not violate any confidentiality. Unfortunately higher education leadership is not always cut and dry or black and white. In some instances you must withhold information for the greater good of the university and it is during these times that I am always conscious of the overarching goal. As long as you have core values and understand that institutional needs sometimes outweigh straightforward answers then your integrity should remain intact.

My First University-Wide Initiative

One of the major components of the OURS program was to identify an Action Learning Project (ALP) that allowed you to: apply the content learned in the courses to a real-life situation, gain institution-wide recognition, and address areas of personal improvement as identified in the 360 individualized assessment. For my ALP project I decided to develop a plan to successfully implement the GradesFirst system at my current institution, Elizabeth City State University (ECSU). GradesFirst was strategically chosen since it would provide great visibility across campus and within the University of North Carolina General Administration (UNC GA), the governing body for all 16 public universities in North Carolina. Although I could have chosen a much smaller project that was less work, I knew that by choosing the implementation of GradesFirst I would be able to: engage in a program that was mandated by UNC GA, speak to the full faculty multiple times a year, have direct contact with the Provost and Vice Chancellor for Academic Affairs, and most of all work on something that would directly benefit students. The main purpose of GradesFirst was to provide a streamlined method for monitoring students' progress in an effort to improve the academic success and retention rates of students. During the year prior to my ALP an attempt to implement GradesFirst failed miserably. The training on the platform was poor, there were numerous technical difficulties and the implementation lacked clear expectations on how GradesFirst was to be utilized by faculty. Since I used GradesFirst in my department and had experienced its value I understood the importance of ensuring this initiative was successful. I believed that a successful implementation of GradesFirst as an early alert warning and advising management system would greatly transform the university. Below I use Kotter's (1995) model to outline how I implemented the GradesFirst initiative.

1. Establishing a Sense of Urgency –Prior to implementing GradesFirst, ECSU's enrollment had dropped by more than 50% over a 6 year period. The reduction in enrollment made it essential that ECSU retained its current student population in order to survive. Using GradesFirst as an early alert warning system that required faculty to issue progress reports for students who were at-risk for failing a course during the 3rd and 7th week of classes would go a long way in increasing retention. In addition, incorporating GradesFirst advising management features provided a way for advisors, students and staff to all stay on the same page regarding a student's overall performance and progress towards degree.

2. Forming a Powerful Guiding Coalition – In order to successfully institute the GradesFirst system at ECSU it was essential that

faculty and staff viewed the upper level administration as support-
ing the initiative. To do this I began by having the Chancellor first
introduce the platform to the entire campus during his State of
the University address. Premiering the technology in this manner
gave him the opportunity to outline his vision for the system and
create a sense of urgency for widespread adoption.

3. Creating a Vision – Creating a simple vision was one of the
toughest parts of implementing the GradesFirst system since it required time and participation from upper level administration. In
order to do this I worked with the administrative team on identifying exactly how the GradesFirst system aligned with the 5 year
strategic plan and refining the vision with input from key constituents.

4. Communicating the Vision – In order to make sure that the vision was communicated often I worked with the Provost to ensure
that I gave updates during every general faculty meeting. I also
had each department name a GradesFirst liaison that was charged
with communicating with their respective departments at each departmental meeting and serving as a champion for this initiative
within their department. The administrative team worked closely with marketing to develop an internal branding for the plat-
formthat accurately depicted this initiative. Furthermore, I made
sure that all key stakeholders were able to communicate the vision
through a simple elevator pitch that clearly explained why the
initiative was important.

5. Empowering Others to Act on the Vision – The introduction of
a new technology is one of the major obstacles that could have

impeded the progress of the GradesFirst initiative. To address this potential roadblock the team developed a well-thought out training program that included face-to-face training, online tutorial videos, one-page help guides and a designated email for questions and concerns.

6. Planning for and Creating Short-term Wins – A phased approach was used to implement the GradesFirst system with short-term wins built in. The first short-term win that was realized was the implementation of athletic travel letters which greatly reduced the number of emails faculty received for student athlete absences. Increases in semester to semester and year to year retention rates were also used as a way to illustrate short-term wins.

7. Consolidating Improvements and Producing Still More Change – The GradesFirst system is a very sophisticated piece of technology that is constantly evolving as time goes by. The team acknowledged wins as they came but always focused on continuing to push the boundaries of the technology; constantly exploring opportunities for improvement. Continuously using a phased approach with built in assessments and refinement points was one way the team ensured that the GradesFirst initiative would continue to progress and evolve.

8. Institutionalizing New Approaches – In order to institutionalize GradesFirst into the ECSU culture it was essential that the administrative team identified ways that the platform could be used to simplify existing protocols and procedures. Expanding the platform to Financial Aid, Student Accounts and the Registrar's Office was one way additional users were brought into the system.

The GradesFirst project was launched campus-wide in 2014 and is still being used three years later. Faculty participation in the GradesFirst project has been outstanding with all of the Progress Report Campaigns having faculty response rates of 90% or higher. In June 2015 ECSU joined the Education Advisory Board Student Success Collaborative (SSC), the company that acquired GradesFirst. ECSU has branded the SSC platform into its own E4U Platform (Engaging, Enriching, Empowering, Effective) and launched the new E4U platform on March 7, 2016. In 2016 ECSU was featured on EAB's website and in print ads for its outstanding work on faculty engagement and in 2017 the university received the EAB Collaborative Citizenship Award for its commitment to student success. Although not solely a result of E4U, one of the greatest accomplishments ECSU has experienced has been a 5% increase in the freshman retention rate from 2015 to 2016.

Institutional-Wide Initiatives on My Journey

After successfully launching the GradesFirst/E4U platform I began to think about what other areas on campus needed to be refined in order to enhance student success. Somehow during the implementation of GradesFirst/E4U I became extremely interested in increasing Student Success and was motivated by how changes in faculty and advisor behavior could greatly improve the student experience. It was clear to me that we needed a comprehensive plan to truly increase student retention and improve timely degree completion for all students. There is no doubt that technology played a vital role in improving the timely degree completion of students; however, academic advising remained one of the most critical components of any student success initiative. Improving the academic advising seemed like a natural next step in the development process. Understanding that this was an area of opportunity I wrote and secured a $50,000 grant from UNC GA to enhance the academic advising at ECSU. Led by faculty, an Academic Advising Advisory Board developed a uniform advising protocol that outlined how students and advisors used E4U to schedule appointments, document meetings, and store advising records. Advising training modules were developed that helped advisors understand academic policies, counsel at-risk students, and navigate the various technologies used during the advising process. Establishing a standard advising protocol helped bring consistency to a students' advising experience with the ultimate goal of improving retention, persistence and graduation rates. When you find an area that you are passionate about think about how initiatives can be linked together to increase their institutional impact.

Three months after I was received the advising grant I was approached by the Chancellor and the Registrar about implementing the degree audit system DegreeWorks. DegreeWorks allows advisors, and students, to quickly monitor students' progress towards degree completion and easily identify any outstanding requirements. DegreeWorks also provides students and advisors an opportunity to explore how existing credits can be applied to possible alternative majors when considering a change of major. The DegreeWorks implementation project was not on my radar at all because I was already quite busy, I had just secured a $50,000 grant to improve advising and although I had full release time I was still serving as department chair. After seeing the demonstration of DegreeWorks and how both advisors and students would be able to instantly see what courses students had completed and what courses were still needed I immediately understood how using DegreeWorks would greatly improve a time-consuming manual process for faculty and students. Although I realized that working on the DegreeWorks project would increase my work-load I remained flexible and went full steam with the implementation project. As leaders we are often asked to serve on numerous committees or head projects when we are overloaded. Although you might be tempted to say no, when you have a vision and are presented with opportunities to carry out your vision it is important to invest your time and energy into those initiatives.

While I was enrolled in the OURS program I remembered reading an article about how the length of time to graduation was an issue that was causing Americans to question the true value of a college degree (Heller, 2012). The article went on to say how only 57% of American students would go on to complete a four-year degree within six years which was not a very encouraging statistic. A friend of mine worked in the Nebraska state system and told me how the state of Nebraska had reduced the required credits for graduation to 120 for all academic programs in the state university system. While the University of North Carolina system had begun a preliminary investigation to do the same a few priors there was little talk about moving forward. Although E4U and academic advising reform addressed communication between faculty, students and advisors, I realized that reducing curricular barriers was an essential component of improving student success. During the Fall 2016 semester I led an initiative to reduce the general education curriculum from 46 – 48 credits to 35 credits. I later went on to get 91% of the faculty to approve an across the board reduction in the number of credits required for graduation from 124 – 128 credits to 120 credits for all majors. In Fall 2017 a new initiative, 15 to Finish, that focused on students enrolling in 15 credit hours each semester in order to graduate in four years was launched at ECSU. Having been exposed to research on curriculum reform and having first-hand knowledge of a state system that had reduced their curriculums was crucial in this situation. As leaders it is important to be well versed on higher education trends and look for ways where those programs or initiatives can be implemented on your campus.

Transitioning to Senior Leadership

I wish I could say that I was thinking about improving Student Success for years and the work I have been involved in was part of a grand master plan but the truth is it wasn't. Before beginning my OURS Action Learning Project I was completely content serving as Chair of the Department of Mathematics and Computer Science and never really thought of advancing to a senior leadership position. My vision to improve Student Success was never planned out but just simply developed as I went along in the process. With each success I became more excited about how an initiative could literally transform a student's life by from potentially reducing the amount of money they owed in student loans because they graduated faster to helping them secure an internship because they received proper advisement. I was not looking for a new role because of power or prestige but I did desire a title such as Coordinator of Student Success so faculty would understand the university's commitment to Student Success. I realized that my work on the numerous projects was clearly noticed by the Provost when one day I received a call to serve as Interim Associate Vice Chancellor for Academic Affairs. I was blown away when I received the call but knew this was my chance to be in a position to further push all of the initiatives that I envisioned for improving student success. Since I was only appointed as Interim I knew I would have to apply for the position in order to become permanent. What I later realized was that everything I had done up until that point had prepared me for this new position. Although I prepared for the interview and knew I had an advantage because I had served in the position for 6 months and understood what it entailed it didn't matter because I was ready. When interviewing it is important for leaders to articulate their successes and clearly explain how the experiences along their leadership journey have prepared them for the job they are seeking.

As indicated previously I have held many leadership roles in my lifetime. I believe that the leadership roles I have had have provided me an opportunity to see the world from a different perspective. As a faculty member you are often focused on your courses and how your students perform on day to day task; however, as an administrator you see the inner workings of the university from a completely different vantage point. My current understanding of key dynamics such as how declines in enrolment can lead to employee layoffs have made me even more passionate about ensuring that the university is successful.. I also recognize that some things in higher education are political and that is important that you are cognizant of what is going on in local and state politics. Senior administration requires a lot of passion and is probably an extremely difficult job if one is motivated by power and prestige. Although my job is quite time consuming it is also extremely rewarding and I wake up each day with a renewed spirit about how my small contribution has the potential to truly change a student's life.

References

Heller, Donald. (2012). "Not what it used to be: American universities represent declining value for money to their students." *The Economist*. 409(8813), pp. 29-30. Retrieved from http://www.economist.com/news/united-states/21567373-american-universities-represent-declining-value-money-their-students-not-what-it

Kotter, J.P. (1995). "Leading Change: Why Transformation Efforts Fail." *Harvard Business Review*, March-April: 59-67.

PART III

LYNCHPIN LEADERSHIP

CHAPTER 11

My Personal Academic Leadership Journey

Cleo Hughes Darden, PhD

As I reflect on my academic career, I realize that my leadership journey began when I joined the Department of Biology at Morgan State University (MSU) as an Assistant Professor twenty-five years ago. Twenty-five years ago, MSU was mainly a teaching university with a small number of funded research projects in the sciences with an undeveloped research infrastructure. Improving the research infrastructure and recruiting research faculty were part of the University's strategic plan to become a Doctoral Research University. As a member of a small group of research faculty recruited to participate in developing the research infrastructure in the Department of Biology, we wrote several individual and collaborative grants, to fund and build active and competitive research programs: NSF-RUI, NIH-MBRS, NIH-RIMI, and NIH-RCMI. As PI and Co-PI on several funded research projects, in areas of Plant Molecular Biology, Cellular and Molecular Biology, and Cell Signaling, I began developing relevant leadership skills to manage my active research laboratory that included students, staff, and faculty collaborators.

For example, in my new role as Assistant Professor and Researcher, I realized that essential leadership skills were required to manage an active research laboratory efficiently. Through trial and error and talking with senior faculty and administrators, I learned critical leadership skills in order for my laboratory to function optimally. Some of these skills were: developing scientific strategies for experiments; motivating students, staff, and collaborating faculty; managing grant budgets; mentoring students, and acquiring patience with research students during training (1). Other acquired skills were facilitating effective teamwork, managing team conflicts, negotiating with students and staff, and dealing with difficult staff (2). These leadership skills took time and effort to acquire and, on many occasions, new strategies for managing and facilitating teamwork had to be developed as personnel changed in the laboratory. The changes in personnel led to updating and acquiring additional leadership skills since Higher Education is a continually changing environment (3).

Simultaneously, I was unaware that the PI and Program Director of Maximizing Academic Research Careers program (MARC) observed how I managed my laboratory and maintained continuous funding (three grants from NSF and NIH) over the past five years. Also, the Co-PI and Co-Program Director decided to retire. Therefore, I was asked to serve as Co-PI for the program. As Co-PI, I would interact mainly with students and mentors and organize events for the program. During the time I was serving as Co-PI and Co- Program Director, I was promoted to Associate Professor with tenure. Also, forty students graduated from the program, and eighty-seven percent of the students had plans to enroll and complete graduate and/or professional degrees.

The MARC program was in the last year of the funding cycle. Since my tenure as MARC Co-PI was successful, I was appointed the PI and Director of the MARC program (2006) and charged to write the proposal for the "New MARC program" at MSU which began in 2009. The decision was somewhat difficult because I would spend much less time training and mentoring students in my laboratory. Furthermore, it would be challenging to write and submit papers for publication and grants for funding in order to to maintain my actively funded laboratory.

This was a major challenge for me because I had success over the past thirteen years in maintaining an actively funded research laboratory and training over twenty students in the research areas of Plant Molecular Biology, Cellular, and Molecular Biology, and Cell Signaling. These students participated in several different research training programs such as NSF-RUI, NIH-MARC, NIH-MBRS-RISE, HBCU-UP, NIH-BRIDGES, and NSF-LSAMP. In addition to the students in research training programs, some students volunteered to work in my laboratory. These research students presented their work at local and national meetings and co-authored several abstracts and some manuscripts. Most of these students are currently working in several different professions in science-related fields including scientists, medical doctors, research/lab technicians, secondary school teachers, and entrepreneurs. Despite my early successes as a faculty researcher, I knew that this new role would be a different leadership experience for me where my focus would be on the success of the students.

Once the new MARC program was funded in 2009, I embarked on a new leadership role at MSU as Program Director for the program. As Program Director, I was accountable to ten trainees every year, ten faculty mentors, program administration, University administration, internal and external advisory committees and the NIH-NIGMS. Learning how to manage all aspects of the MARC program was somewhat challenging at times and was a learning experience. Hiring the Program Coordinator and selecting the MARC trainees were crucial for the success of the program. Since this program's intended outcome was successful enrollment into Ph.D. or MD/ Ph.D. programs, it was essential that we select students that have the potential of fulfilling the goal of the program. Also, it was essential to know the students, their strengths and weaknesses, and learn how to motivate trainees to pursue Ph.D. or MD/ Ph.D. degrees when they became discouraged. Even though there were challenges, there were a number of rewarding experiences especially when the trainees achieved their goals. Since 2006, I have been the MARC Program Director at MSU and a total of thirty-five students completed the program. Eighty-five percent of the students either completed the MS degree, currently enrolled in MS, MD/PhD, and Ph.D. programs, or are currently employed in the health and/or science-related jobs.

As I reflect on my decision to become MARC Program Director (PD), it was bittersweet. I enjoyed working with the students and assisting them in launching their careers in science. Also, I improved my leadership skills and provided service to the School of Computer Mathematical and Natural Sciences (SCMNS) and MSU. However, I was in a position where there were limited publishing opportunities, since it was difficult to continue writing research grants to sustain my research laboratory. It was also difficult to publish in student training during the time I was Program Director. Therefore, my level of publications decreased. In hindsight, I would have identified more opportunities to publish and through collaborative effort conduct science education research to understand student learning and to improve student knowledge retention. The leadership skills and experience gained as faculty/ researcher and as MARC Program Director were immeasurable.

After nine years as PD of the MARC program, I began thinking more about academic leadership and observing how women leaders at the University were promoted. One of my mentors was a significant supporter of my career aspirations and provided me with different opportunities for growth and development. I observed her leadership style, skills, and her ability to navigate through different challenges in her several roles in upper administration. As I watched her navigate through these different challenges, one observation was clear: the university landscape is always changing and as a leader, one must be prepared for it.

The changing university landscape was evident in the SCMNS and in the Department of Biology in particular. In the Department of Biology, there were several changes in leadership: two Chairs, and two Interim Chairs in six years. The view of the Biology Department by non-biology faculty in the SCMNS and the Dean of the SCMNS was that the Department of Biology was in disarray. To my surprise, I was asked by the Dean of SCMNS to lead the department as Interim Chair in January of 2013. In the Spring of 2013, I was appointed Chair of the Department of Biology.

Later that same year, an Interim Dean for SCMNS was appointed. My thoughts were, what can I offer to the faculty and students of the department, SCMNS, and the MSU? I understood the culture of the faculty and students, since I spent my entire career here at MSU. I knew ninety percent of the faculty because I served on several committees with most of them, wrote proposals with some of them and developed new courses with others. Therefore, I knew most of the faculty strengths and weaknesses. Also, my Leadership 360 analysis from my direct reports indicated that I am fair, consistent, attentive to viewpoints prior to making decisions, and has a calm and systematic leadership style.

As Chair, thus far, I have had an impact on the faculty and

students within the Department through shared governance which is the delicate balance between faculty and staff participation in planning and decision-making processes. With the assistance of the faculty, the department is in the process of improving the educational and research infrastructure. Therefore, improving the curriculum, teaching, student advising, and mentoring will result in increased retention and graduation rates for the Department, SCMNS, and MSU.

Under my leadership, the Department of Biology has been focused on student success, student research training, instructional delivery improvement, science curriculum through implementation of Vision and Change core concepts and competencies, and faculty development. The department was selected as one of the eight pilot institutions to participate in a Departmental assessment for the Partnership for Undergraduate Life Sciences Education (PULSE) which is a National effort to transform undergraduate Biology Education. Other departmental initiatives: BIOL 101 Course redesign, BIOL 105/106 and BIOL 310 redesign, and develop courses to improve the biology curriculum. There are other initiatives that are in progress.

In addition, I actively participated in programs, that promote increased student engagement through active learning, and the infusion of computation and cultural competency into STEM courses through the Teaching to Increase Diversity and Equity in STEM (Morgan TIDES) program which is an interdisciplinary initiative funded by AAC&U and the Hemsley Foundation. The Department of Biology at MSU is a work in progress and my goal is to continue the momentum of working in teams which was difficult early in my tenure as Chair. It is my hope that we continue to become more like a family of faculty working together to support the students and each other.

Furthermore, I am involved in other activities such as student training. I was appointed as the Coordinator for the Louis Stokes Alliance for Minority Participation (LSAMP) program whose main goal is to increase underrepresented students who complete baccalaureate degrees in science, technology, engineering, and mathematics (STEM), along with increasing the number of underrepresented students who successfully enter and complete graduate programs. I am also the Co-Director of the Student Training Core for the Building Infrastructure Leading to Diversity/ A Student-Centered Entrepreneurship Development (BUILD/ ASCEND) program which has a similar goal but focuses on underrepresented students who are interested in biomedical and behavioral sciences.

More recently, as Chair, I have been involved in one faculty development and two student training grants. Since my time as Program Director, I have learned that it is very important to find opportunities to publish. I am one of the co-authors on a student training grant paper (BUILD/ASCEND), co-author on a course redesign paper (BIOL 310 Course), and first author on a book chapter (TIDES) about faculty development. I plan to continue to find opportunities to publish with the goal of obtaining full professor and other leadership positions.

In conclusion, I would like to thank the NSF/Opportunities for UnderRepresented Scholars (OURS) program, for providing me the opportunity to participate in the OURS program and for continuous training through the Fielding Conclave Leadership Academy. The information discussed was timely and further prepared me for the challenges I am encountering as Chair of the largest department in the SCMNS. I am grateful for all my experiences as faculty researcher, Program Director and Chairperson because they have made me aware that leadership is challenging and rewarding and that one of the major goals of a leader is to empower others.

References

Chuang, S-F. (2013). "Essential Skills for Leadership Effectiveness in Diverse Workplace Development." *Online Journal Education and Development*. 6:1. 2013.

Gmelch, WH. and Buller, JL. (2015). *Building Academic Leadership Capacity: A Guide to Best Practices*, Jossey-Bass: A Wiley Brand.

Guberman, J., Saks, J., Shapiro B., and Torchia, M. (2006). *Making the Right Moves: A Practical Guide to Scientific Management for Postdocs and New Faculty Burroughs*. Wellcome Fund, Howard Hughes Medical Institute.

CHAPTER 12

Making You a By-Product of It!
Lisa D. Brown, PhD

As a young new Assistant Professor, I entered the arena of academia full of energy and ready to take on the task of riding the wave towards promotion and tenure. I had already gained some teaching experience while teaching as both a graduate student and as a postdoctoral fellow. As a graduate student, I served as a Teaching Assistant for several courses. While these teaching experiences were not independent and required mentoring by a professor, it did allow me to start the process of organizing my thoughts, practicing my verbal communication skills, and implementing teaching pedagogies. As a postdoctoral fellow, I decided to put my toes in the water and try my hand at lecturing at several community colleges. A part time adjunct teaching position at a 4-year university and finally an adjunct position at my current institution followed. Given the current climate in which entry level positions in academia were on the decline, these teaching experiences, along with my research experience as a postdoc, would give me some value as I sought out to gain a tenure-track position in academia. I now had the confidence that I needed to transition from a postdoctoral fellow to a tenure-track professor in academia. In fact, my current institution thought that I was ready to make the transition and offered me a full-time tenure track position. I have been at Morgan State University ever since and absolutely love teaching at an HBCU. Besides the regular teaching, I am pouring into my students all of the things (advice, tough love, and the "it takes a village" mentality) that I wished my undergraduate professors had invested in me.

Little did I know that this road to tenure and promotion included what is known as the "three legged stool" with one leg each representing teaching, scholarly activities (more specifically, an active academic research program), and service to the institution. The importance of these three components varies widely depending on the institution and their particular requirements for tenure. Some institutions place more emphasis on research, depending on their Carnegie classification. Others institutions, such as small liberal arts colleges, place more emphasis on teaching. The assumption is that everyone knows about this concept and understands the relative importance of these three components at their particular institution. I had become familiar and comfortable with the idea of research and teaching, but no one nor any of my experiences had prepared me for the third leg of the stool, service. Service comes in various forms: service to the department, service to your School, service to the University, and service to the community in general. And as a new Assistant Professor, there was an unspoken expectation that I was to engage in some sort of service at all of these levels.

If we consider the metaphor of a stool, the stool is not level unless all three legs are equal in length. Similarly, I was expected to engage in a balancing act of engaging in teaching, research, and service equally. All three of these components are taken into consideration for promotion and tenure. By my third year, I became overwhelmed with this balancing act and started to lose focus. Many times, my "junior" status as an Assistant Professor meant that I was "voluntold" (told that I was volunteered) for a committee. It is somewhat hard to tell higher administration, your Dean or your Departmental Chairperson that you do not want to serve, especially when the service is pitched as a unique opportunity and that you were specifically chosen from amongst many. I persisted and was finally able to get some grant funding for my research, train a number of undergraduate students in my research laboratory, develop and teach a course that I could call my own, and serve on a number of departmental and School committees. It was difficult and consumed all of my time, but I persisted and finally earned a promotion and tenure. Even after achieving tenure and a promotion to Associate Professor, the balancing act continued.

What I learned from the experience and what I wished I had done from day one was to choose my service activities wisely. I wish that I had limited my service to those activities that would benefit me in a more direct way. It's ok to say "no", especially if you are having a hard time managing the responsibilities that you already have. Unfortunately, the more times you say "yes" or the more times you allow yourself to be "voluntold", the more times you are requested to serve on additional service activities because you have shown yourself to be a team player. Thus, it becomes a never-ending cycle. Once I obtained tenure, I decided to be more strategic in the service activities that I engaged in at work. When a service activity did not benefit me directly, I simply responded with "I'm sorry but, that does not work for me". It was an easier way of saying no because I just didn't want to and placed more emphasis on not having the time to fit it into my already packed schedule. Of course, when someone from higher administration asks you to serve on a committee or be a part of a special project, you have to be more careful in your response as it may set the tone for how they view your value to the university in the future.

In 2012, I was having a conversation with my Dean about

the retirement of the Coordinator of our Schools Honors Program. She served a dual role of Coordinator of the Honors Program and also a lecturer in the mathematics department. The Dean kept hinting that I should consider taking on this additional responsibility. Here I was again put in a position where it was hard to say no to your Dean but, at the same time, I was already overwhelmed with teaching and trying to maintain an active research program. The previous Coordinator had left without any established guidelines, courses, or activities for the program. Thus, taking on this position would be a lot of additional work. With funding for research being more difficult to obtain, and as a result, publishing my research findings being harder to do, I decided to take some time to consider if taking on this new task would allow me to continue being active in scholarly activities. After careful consideration, I came to the realization that this could be an opportunity to switch from engagement in a traditional scientific research program to scholarly activities in STEM education. This would allow me to develop and teach new courses specifically for the Honors Program, publish STEM education research, and provide a huge service to my School and the University Honors College. More importantly, being the Coordinator of our Schools' Honors Program would allow me to develop my leadership skills and provide me with significant visibility. In essence, I could make ME a byproduct of the Honors Program. I immediately set out to redesign the two Honors courses that already existed from simple seminar courses with guest speakers who spoke about their careers, to courses that were more focused in the development of critical thinking skills. Beyond developing these two courses, it was quite difficult to get buy in from my colleagues and to get support from my Dean for further curriculum development and financial support for activities for the Honors Program. It was also proving to be difficult to balance my duties to my department as the Associate Chair, and my duties as the Honors Program Coordinator.

My participation in the Opportunities for UnderRepresented Scholars (OURS) Fellowship Program in 2015 was quite timely as this program focused on academic leadership and helped me to discover and develop "ME", both personally and professionally. My first task was to assess and explore my work style and relationship building behaviors through completion of the DISC assessment tool. The DISC (dominance, inducement, submission, and compliance) tool allowed me to analyze how I relate to others, respond to challenges, rules and procedures as a leader. A Leadership Effectiveness Analysis (LEA) questionnaire was completed by a number of my colleagues (bosses, peers, and direct reports) to assess how they perceived my leadership role. Together both tools were effective in giving me a complete view of my strengths and weaknesses and areas that would be most beneficial to focus in in terms of demonstrating and showcasing my leadership potential. Part of the Fellowship Program required the completion of an Action Learning Project (ALP). This project would allow me to 1) apply what I learned in the Academic Leadership Program and, 2) develop those areas of weakness as outlined by the DISC and LEA assessment tools to an on-the-job project. Since I was having difficulty in getting the Honors Program off the ground, it was logical and made sense for me to use the Honors Program as my ALP. I was able to identify key stakeholders, key people who could help me implement my vision, short- and long-term goals for the program, a timetable for implementation, and a plan for making the program and me more visible. I also became more focused and deliberate in my short-term and long-term goals for my personal and professional growth.

I was able to develop some very specific leadership and organizational skills, utilize them to gain some momentum in the development of the Honors Program from the ground up, and demonstrate that I could work independently and contribute to the overall mission of Morgan State University. The central theme for Honors courses was development of critical thinking and leadership skills. Two more courses (for a total of 4 courses) were developed at each academic level. The Honors Program became a line item for discussion on the agenda at the School Chairs' meeting, and a newsletter was developed that showcased the accomplishments of the Honors students. This newsletter is distributed campus-wide and via the newly created Honors Program website that is a subpage of the School website. In terms of STEM education research, I am assessing and measuring the development of critical thinking skills at different levels of completion of the Honors courses. This focus on critical thinking skills has also allowed me to expand the idea to assessment with various types of course interventions to a broader group of students.

In order to ease this transition from scientific research to a focus on the Honors Program and STEM education research, I have learned to leverage my newly discovered leadership role to get release time, some financial assistance from my Dean, and visibility amongst the other leaders on campus. I am now able to be more selective about the types of service activities I engage in and have more influence on a broader scale. I am pleased to say that I have made "ME a byproduct of "IT" and am looking forward towards another promotion and a trajectory towards a higher administration position.

CHAPTER 13

Leading from the Middle

Triscia W. Hendrickson, PhD

While I was sitting on a stone wall outside of the Math and Science building at the University of the Virgin Islands (UVI) complaining about the level of rigor in the Biology program, one of the older nursing students said to me, "*To whom much is given, much is expected.*" That quote from the New Testament has stuck with me ever since and whenever I think about my career path and what I hope to accomplish in the future, I remember that great gifts mean great responsibilities.

My path has been dictated by a need to create more and better opportunities for those who are coming after me, while ensuring that my peers and I are in the best possible position to do the most good. I've always been driven to do things the right way or to bring balance and fairness to whatever endeavor I'm involved in. As a young child, I got in trouble a lot for correcting adults. If someone said the wrong thing, I'd call him or her out. If they mispronounced a word, I'd correct them. Although this behavior was frowned on, I was always encouraged to strive for excellence. One could say that education is my family's business.

I come from a family of educators: my grandmother was a Home Economics teacher, all of my father's siblings taught at one point or another in their lives, my father was a teacher for short while, and my mother is a high school English teacher. However, I had no interest in becoming an educator until I was in college. I have always loved science; the fact that science demands that one asks questions about how things work piqued my interest. I became fascinated with biology and physics in high school, thanks to great teachers. So when I enrolled in college, I chose biology as my major, thinking that I would go on to become a physician. However, as I matriculated through college, I became increasingly disturbed by the fact that none of my biology professors looked like me, despite my institution being classified as a Historically Black University and despite it being located in the Caribbean. The lack of Black professors in my discipline led me to consider becoming a college professor. Although, I received a solid foundation at the undergraduate level, I felt that my professors could not relate to me because they were all Caucasian or Asian. And so, I started to think about what it would take to change the face of STEM faculty, particularly at Historically Black Colleges and Universities (HBCUs). I realized then that I needed to get a PhD. Prior to beginning college, I had never met a Black person with a PhD in the sciences. Fortunately, at the time there were two Black chemistry professors at UVI who were also alumni of the university, and they served as a source of inspiration for me. I inquired about their path to becoming college professors and found that after earning their PhDs, they returned to UVI with the hope of making a difference. So I embarked on a journey to pursue a PhD with the intention of returning to my alma mater to teach biology and mentor students like myself. Simply knowing that someone who once sat where I was now sitting and who had successfully travelled a path that I was considering was instrumental in my decision making process. It made me believe that it was possible to get a PhD and return to change the face of science at my institution.

My preparation included a two-year fellowship in the Maximizing (then Minority) Access to Research Careers (MARC) program, which along with a summer research training program at Purdue University gave me the research background necessary to be a successful applicant to a graduate program. I chose to attend Emory University to pursue my PhD, and I probably would not have made it through grad school without my support network of Black women. These women, who were grad students like me, talked me off the ledge when I wanted to quit grad school to become an interior designer (gasp!). They encouraged me when I was feeling homesick and missing my family. They helped to keep me sane when things weren't going as expected in the lab. They surrounded and lifted me with their Black Girl Magic. Years later, I realized that I did the same for those coming after me, but it didn't occur to me then that I was a peer mentor. This was a key lesson on my journey: treat everyone with kindness and compassion; you never know what impact this may have on their lives. Had I simply buried myself in the lab and not taken the time to focus on the spiritual and social aspects of myself I would have missed out on forming deep and lasting relationships with a group of amazing Black women.

After completing my graduate studies, I was invited to give a research talk at the University of the Virgin Islands. It was an honor to be invited back and I was even more surprised when one of my professors, who had retired years before, attended the seminar. After the seminar we chatted for a while and one of the comments that she made about my talk was that I spoke too fast. It quickly became apparent, based on that conversation and others with professors who taught me when I was a student, that if I were to return to UVI as a junior faculty member I would never be treated as their equal. While this was a painful realization, it allowed me the freedom to consider other options. For five years, I had been telling myself that once I completed my PhD, I would return to the Virgin Islands. Now I was no longer constrained to that narrow path. Instead, I entered the FIRST post-doctoral program, where I began learning how to be an effective teacher while continuing my research training. Also during this time, I began considering where I might be most effective at changing the face of STEM and decided that a small primarily teaching institution would be ideal. My teaching experience during the FIRST post-doc was at Morehouse College, an all-male, Historically Black, Liberal Arts College in southwest Atlanta. Initially, I was apprehensive about teaching at an all-male institution, primarily because I was certain that my calling was to educate Black girls and women. Nevertheless, I continued my training at Morehouse and during that time I worked with someone who to this day continues to mentor me. Toward the end of my second year as a post-doc, a position became available in the Biology department at Spelman College, the all-female, Historically Black, Liberal Arts College across the street from Morehouse. I just knew that God had created that opportunity for me, so I applied but indicated on my cover letter that if offered the position I would need a deferment for one year to complete my post-doc. Around the same time, a position also opened in the Biology department at Morehouse College and I was encouraged by my mentor to apply, which I did. However, I was certain that I was going to end up at Spelman, so you can just imagine my disappointment when I was told that although I made it to the top list of candidates, they needed someone who could start immediately, and because I had not completed my post-doc, I was no longer being considered for the position. After all, I had convinced myself that my mission was to educate those who looked like me – Black women. But then Morehouse made me an offer, and they agreed to my terms, I would be allowed a year to complete my post-doc. So although I did not get what at that time I considered to be my dream job, the fact that Morehouse was willing to wait one year so that I could strengthen my research foundation spoke volumes of the type of support that would be waiting for me when I joined the faculty there. So I said yes. This was another key lesson on my journey: Approach life with an open mind while remaining focused on the goal and use disappoints as opportunities to consider other, and most times better, options. Had I been single-minded about my career options, I would have returned to UVI to become a junior faculty member who would have been regarded as a student. Likewise, if I had not been open to the idea that I could be a successful female professor in a predominantly male environment, I would not have ended up at Morehouse College.

Since joining the faculty at Morehouse College, I have been successful in advancing my research program while serving the College and my profession. This has led to opportunities to teach instructors in Tanzania and Ghana how to teach Cell Biology and to present my work at national and international conferences. But most importantly, I have been able to train many students from Morehouse College and Spelman College in my lab. These students have gone on to pursue advanced degrees and many of them are now engaged in STEM careers. My goal is still to impact STEM education, but in addition to that, it is important that I make a contribution to the efforts to diversify the STEM workforce. According to the 2010 US Census African Americans make up approximately 13% of the US population, but only 3% of the STEM workforce, as reported by US News and World Report. We are significantly underrepresented in STEM.

Historically Black Colleges and Universities (HBCUs) have always out performed predominantly White institutions when it comes to training and preparing Black students for graduate and professional studies; therefore, I am in the perfect space to contribute to the efforts to broaden participation in STEM. Since joining the faculty of Morehouse College, I've trained over 30 students in my research lab, received funding from the National Institutes of Health, the National Science Foundation, and private organizations. I've published peer-reviewed articles and moved up through the ranks of academia. And although many of my colleagues are doing the same, we have not significantly moved the needle on diversifying the STEM workforce.

This led me to the realization that changes that are being made by individual faculty members are incremental and only transformative change can truly lead to broader participation in STEM. Transformative change begins with institutional change, and so in an effort to broaden participation in STEM, I have been engaged in efforts at my institution to increase and improve opportunities for students and faculty.

As a result of this focus on broadening participation, I've been presented with opportunities to serve in various leadership roles on my campus. In these roles I have learned many valuable lessons.

As a junior faculty member, I was eager to make a contribution to the institution and at the time I felt that I was best equipped to do so by joining the Faculty Research Committee. After one year on the committee, I was elected to serve as its chair. The Faculty Research Committee was composed of faculty from all over the campus who all had different ideas about research at the institution. Therefore, I had to work with my committee to create a collaborative environment that fostered research development on the campus. One of the main initiatives that I led while serving on the Faculty Research Committee was the Faculty Release Time Grants (FRTG). Faculty members would submit proposals to the Faculty Research Committee and if funded the FRTG would allow the faculty member to be released from teaching one course for a semester. At an institution where the full teaching load is three courses per semester, these FRTG were highly sought after. Some of my duties as the chair of the committee included overseeing the review of proposals, notifying colleagues of the status of their proposals, and maintaining an objective atmosphere among the committee members. Having to tell someone that her proposal was not funded was extremely difficult, especially if that person is a close colleague. Equally difficult was the prospect of meeting with someone that I barely knew to explain why his proposal was denied. Being chair of the Faculty Research Committee taught me how to bring faculty from different disciplines together to form a cohesive unit and that it is much easier to engage with others if you approach them with sincerity and a willingness to listen.

Several years ago a group of faculty at my institution began collaborating on a proposal for a MARC U-STAR program. My initial role in the project was to design a course that would allow students to get an authentic research experience early in their matriculation. This was well suited for me because I was training students in my lab and I was also teaching a laboratory course which could easily be converted into a "research classroom" course. The proposal was funded and we began training students; however two years into the project we underwent a leadership reorganization and I was asked to step in as the co-Director of the program. In this capacity, I designed and implemented a mentoring curriculum for the program and assisted the director with the overall administration of the program. Two years later the director assumed more a leadership role in the administration and was unable to continue with the directorship, at which time I became the director of the program and was responsible for all aspects of the program, including overseeing the training of 10 students, managing the administration of the grant, supervising the program assistant, and coordinating the faculty mentors. Although I was initially reluctant to assume a full leadership of the program I quickly realized that my training had prepared me for this. The lesson here is to be willing to step into unfamiliar spaces. Today, I am still more comfortable in my research lab working with students, or in a classroom than in a conference room, but knowing that my efforts allow students to be better prepared to graduate school and that this work will result in the STEM workforce being more diverse serves as a constant source of inspiration.

This desire to see more individuals from groups that are underrepresented in the sciences propelled me to say yes when I was asked to serve as the Interim Director of Research and Sponsored Programs and in that role I have been involved in facilitating proposal development with faculty at Morehouse College and fostering collaborations between Morehouse and other institutions. The lessons I learned about coalition building have served me well as I begin implementing a faculty development program for junior faculty in STEM disciplines. The lessons that I learned while implementing the mentoring and training initiatives of the

MARC U-STAR program have allowed me to successfully implement proposal development and grant management training for principal investigators. Most importantly, serving on various committees and leadership initiatives across my institution has taught me to be willing to work with "unlikely" allies, for they may end up being your strongest champions.

And so, as I reflect on my journey thus far, I am reminded of what my fellow student said to me years ago at our alma mater by the sea: "to whom much is given, much is expected." We have been given many opportunities and much more is expected of us as we continue to work toward broadening participation in STEM. Continue to push against the barriers to success, continue to use your disappointments as opportunities, continue to step outside of your comfort zone, continue to expand your network and seek allies, and most importantly, continue to focus on your goals.

PART IV

CAMPUS TRANSFORMATION INITIATIVES

CHAPTER 14

Implementation of a STEM Preprofessional Workshop Series

Amber B. Hodges, PhD

Recognized Need for Increased Student Professional Development

The initial idea of the STEM Preprofessional Workshop Series (STEM PPWS) was birthed from my realization that students in my department needed additional guidance, support and knowledge of the application process when applying for internships and to graduate programs. Students lacked knowledge and preparedness, despite them having earned high grade point averages which resulted in students either putting together poor applications or not applying at all. On numerous occasions this issue was augmented because students missed deadlines due to not submitting mandatory application requirements and/or mismanagement of their time when attempting to complete the application. Additionally, for some students, though they were excelling in their coursework, they were not participating in any co-curricular activities (i.e. research internships), to help them become more prepared to attend graduate school. This subset of students believed that earning good grades would be enough and did not pursue opportunities which would complement what they were leaning in the classroom and subsequently, make them more competitive applicants for graduate programs. However, even students who had both high grade point averages (GPAs) and some research experience still lacked the knowhow required to excel in the application process.

Response to Need for Increased Student Professional Development

To address our student's lack of graduate school application readiness, I formed a Preprofessional Cohort which was comprised of a small group of high achieving psychology majors. We met weekly for one hour and reviewed various aspects of the application process including how to craft a personal statement, how to request a letter of recommendation and how to select internships and graduate programs to apply to. In addition, we discussed time management, their demeanor in class, and how to network both on campus and at professional meetings and seminars. Each week students would have a graduate school readiness assignment to complete and submit to me in which I would provide feedback. Soon these students began completing applications and successfully being accepted to research internships and training programs. For two subsequent academic years, I added two additional cohorts and had similar results. Students were very grateful for the additional guidance and would mention that their friends who were also STEM majors desired the same type of guidance and mentoring from faculty in their departments. More importantly, students who participated in the cohort program were accepted to internships and graduate programs at a higher rate than their peers.

While mentoring two cohorts of students, I also was pursuing a Postdoctoral Certificate in Academic Leadership through the Opportunities for Underrepresented Scholars (OURS) Program. One of the requirements of OURS was that each student had to complete an Action Learning Project (ALP). I thought this would be a good opportunity to develop a structured program that would allow me to reach more STEM majors who were in need of similar guidance and professional development centered around graduate school readiness. Therefore, for my ALP, I initially proposed to develop a STEM Preprofessional Center. The center would serve as an intermediary between the university career center and federally funded biomedical student training programs. STEM students would be able to visit this center and receive training on various aspects of graduate school readiness. An aspect of the ALP was to secure stakeholders including administrators, faculty and staff, representing various units throughout the campus, who could provide support for the project. I met with several stakeholders form units across the campus including the Vice President of Student Affairs, Director of the Career Center, Dean of the Honors College, chairpersons of STEM departments on campus, principal investigators of federally funded student training grants and colleagues in the School of Education. All agreed that this was a much needed service and would greatly benefit our students. Many also thought it would complement training and curriculum already offered through their programs and departments. However, there wasn't funding available to create and staff a STEM Preprofessional Center.

Development and Implementation of the STEM PPWS

Though there was no funding, I remained determined to provide this type of professional development for our students. Therefore, I brainstormed ways in which I could deliver the content that I provided within the weekly cohort meetings, while reaching a larger student population. After listening to a colleague describe a promotion and tenure workshop series offered at her university, I contemplated if I could convert the idea of a STEM Preprofessional Center into a workshop series. And thus, I modified my original proposal of a STEM Preprofessional Career Center into the STEM PPWS. I developed content and material to be presented to the participants, as much of it was based on the earlier cohort meetings and assignments.

The STEM PPWS has two aims. The first is to provide professional development for students by building upon and complementing existing retention programs and research training programs. The second aim is to provide co-curricular support services for STEM majors to encourage them to apply to STEM external internships and graduate programs. The first year of the STEM PPWS, workshops were held monthly during the academic year and covered a specific graduate school readiness topic each month. Examples of the schedule and monthly graduate school readiness topics can be found below in Figure 1.

Figure 1: Sample STEM PPWS Schedule and Topics

Workshop #	Date	Topic
2	Nov-15	Pursuing Research Internships/Graduate Programs
3	Dec-15	How to craft your personal statement

After attending all of the workshops, it was expected that students would have improved graduate school readiness, an increased understanding of graduate school culture and numerous tools they can use to successfully apply for STEM internships and graduate programs. The content of each workshop built upon what was presented and discussed in the previous workshop. The workshop series has a curriculum which includes assignments given during each workshop (with the exception of the last) and each assignment is reviewed at the beginning of the subsequent workshop.

The first academic year, I offered six workshops, three in the fall semester and the remaining during the spring semester. I was able to capitalize on the relationships I formed with several of the stakeholders I listed earlier for recruitment efforts. I sent an email to my stakeholders as well as additional faculty and staff, describing the workshop series, with a copy of the flier for the first workshop attached. I requested they distribute the information to students in their programs and departments. Fortunately, they were willing and strongly encouraged their students to attend. I also sent out the fliers to students in my classes and departments. Also, since the workshops were held in the evening, due to my relationship with the Dean of the Honors College, I asked the honors program to sponsor dinner (i.e. pizza and soda) for the students who attended, which served as an additional incentive for students to participate. The first workshop was held in October 2014 and the topic was "How to become a Competitive Applicant". Though I believed in the importance of the STEM PPWS, I was unsure if many students would attend. I was pleasantly surprised when over 30 students attended the first workshop. After the first workshop, several students came up to me and told me they learned a lot from attending and were going to begin incorporating aspects of what was discussed into their application process. The rest of the workshops were also well attended, averaging 25 students each time. Students began inviting peers who they thought would benefit from the information as well as talking about what they were learning with faculty. As a result of attending the first workshop series, several students successfully applied and were accepted to graduate programs. They attributed their successful applications to skills learned in the workshop series.

With the success of the first workshop series, I was asked by several students and faculty to conduct a second workshop series the next academic year. I agreed, but I also wanted to formally evaluate the effectiveness of the STEM PPWS. Specifically, I decided to begin to collect data from the students who attended the workshops. The aim of this data collection was three-fold. The first was to understand if attending the STEM PPWS increased STEM self-efficacy, STEM career aspirations and STEM persistence in participants. The second was to measure if there was increased knowledge and understanding of STEM graduate school readiness content after attending a workshop in the STEM PPWS. Finally, I wanted to determine if there was a positive correlation between students who attended workshops and those who applied to STEM graduate programs and internships. Data collection consisted of administering a pretest and posttest prior to the first workshop and immediately following the final workshop respectively. Additionally, content specific pretests and posttests were administered prior to and immediately following each workshop that centered on specific graduate school readiness skills. The data collection method is depicted below.

Figure 2: Diagram of Data Collection Schedule to Quantify Effectiveness of STEM PPWS

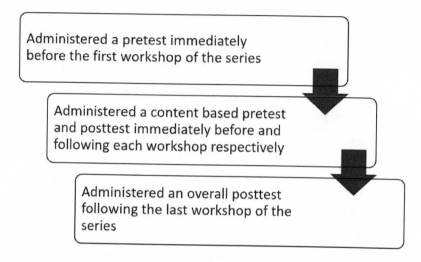

Data collection also allowed us to generate a demographic profile of workshop participants. Approximately 80% of workshop participants grade point averages were between 3.0 and 4.0 and two-thirds of the participants reported participating in a research program or internship. Additionally, 59% reported participating in a professional development activity previously, with several reporting attendance at one or more workshops in the STEM PPWS the prior year. Additionally, early data indicated that students reported benefits from attending even one workshop. For example, when asked to rate their level of agreement to statements such as "I have the ability to successfully apply for a STEM internship/ graduate program" or "I know what type of information to include when writing a personal statement", workshop participants reported significantly higher posttest scores compared to pretest scores. This indicates that attending the workshop increased their knowledge and confidence in various components of graduate school readiness.

Campus Wide Impact and Beyond

Since the inception of the STEM PPWS, it has continued to grow and is now a requirement for students in a student training program as well as freshmen and sophomore honors students in the School of Computer, Mathematical and Natural Sciences. The format has been expanded to be presented in one semester or throughout an academic year. The STEM PPWS has now began to transform undergraduate research training provided by STEM departments and programs on campus, as it is now being used as a professional development mechanism and co-exists with research opportunities already provided by the university. Faculty, staff and administrators support students' participation as they recognize that students are gaining and executing these important yet sometimes intangible skills necessary for them to complete successful applications to STEM internships and graduate programs.

The implementation of the STEM PPWS further supports overall HBCUs efforts to continue to produce competitive STEM majors who pursue STEM graduate and professional degrees. Current efforts focus on providing underrepresented students with research training and mentoring opportunities (Owens, Shelton, Bloom, & Cavil, 2012), but there is not as much emphasis on professional development. Research experiences and mentoring in tangent with professional development provides optimal support and training for students. This is particularly important as research has indicated that while most students are aware of primary criteria used by graduate schools, including grade point average (GPA) and Graduate Record Exam (GRE) scores, students are less aware of importance of second-order criteria, including letters of reference, personal statements or relevant co-curricular experiences (Briihl, 2001). This lack of awareness is critical as graduate programs increasingly rely on these second-order criteria to make admissions decisions. Admission committees cannot reliably discriminate among the growing number of applicants on the basis of their overall GPA and GRE scores alone (Keith-Spiegel et al.,1994). This data further demonstrate the importance of the STEM PPWS and other professional and career development programs that model it, particularly at HBCUs. HBCUs produce more than 25% of black STEM students who go on to earn the doctorate and have had a dominant role in educating and graduating Black and other minority students in STEM (Gasman & Nguyen, 2014; Fiegener & Proudfoot 2013). Future plans include incorporating the STEM PWWS and similar mechanisms in federal grant proposals for student research training grants. Utilizing the STEM PPWS in conjunction with research training and mentoring will boost HBCUs efforts to continue to produce and increase professionals from underrepresented groups in the STEM workforce.

References

Briihl, D. S. (2001). Life after College: Psychology Students' Perceptions of Salary, Business Hiring Criteria, and Graduate Admission Criteria. *North American Journal of Psychology, 3*(2).

Gasman, M., & Nguyen, T. H. (2014). Historically black colleges and universities (HBCUs): Leading our nation's effort to improve the science, technology, engineering, and mathematics (STEM) pipeline. *Texas Education Review, 2* (1) 75-89.

Fiegener, M. K., & Proudfoot, S. L. (2013). Baccalaureate origins of US-trained S&E doctorate recipients. InfoBrief, National Center for Science and Engineering Statistics, Editor, National Science Foundation.

Keith-Spiegel, P., Tabachnick, B. G., & Spiegel, G. B. (1994). When demand exceeds supply: Second-order criteria used by graduate school selection committees. *Teaching of Psychology, 21*(2), 79-81.

Owens, E. W., Shelton, A. J., Bloom, C. M., & Cavil, J. K. (2012). The significance of HBCUs to the production of STEM graduates: Answering the call. *The Journal of Educational Foundations, 26*(3/4), 33.

CHAPTER 15
Campus Transformation at the University of the Virgin Islands: Creativity and Tenacity in Leadership
Camille A. McKayle, PhD

Assuming leadership at a critical juncture

Fall 2012 marked the start of the University of the Virgin Islands' implementation of its *Pathways to Greatness* strategic plan, and also marked my first Fall as Provost at the University of the Virgin Islands. This created an opportunity for me to work through the strategic plan from beginning to end, with the hope of utilizing and honing leadership skills appropriate for the variety of projects that were within the purview of the Provost. Achieving all the goals set out in the plan would certainly change the university, but those that sought to transform the university were the ones that demanded the most from me as a leader. Through this process I have come to recognize that attributes that were seemingly just part of my inner makeup played a pivotal role in defining the type of leadership style I would find the most authentic.

The University of the Virgin Islands (UVI) is a Historically Black University in the U.S. Virgin Islands. Chartered in 1962, the University has seen steady growth. Initially, the university awarded Associates of Arts degrees only. The first baccalaureate degree was awarded in 1970, and the first master's degree in 1976.

UVI's *Pathways to Greatness* Strategic Plan would define my first five years as Provost. The plan was created in a participatory manner to guide the institution's focus and growth from

2012 through 2017. As then Dean of the College of Science and Mathematics, I participated in various sessions with persons internal and external to UVI, exploring ways in which the University could become a better version of itself, while propelling forward. I would now have a different role to play.

As Provost, having a bold strategic plan meant that 2012 was the beginning of five project-filled years. Five areas of focus comprised *Pathways to Greatness*, and the two most relevant to the units under the Provost's oversight, Academic Quality and Excellence, and Student Development and Success, included 22 performance goals, with 51 measurable objectives. Though a formidable task, this strategic plan, with its audacious goals, could signal a sea change in the life of the University of the Virgin Islands.

Goals that transform institutions

Institutions are transformed when new degree levels are added. Over thirty-five years had elapsed since the University had last added the first master's degree in 1976. Achieving the *Pathways to Greatness* goal to "develop and implement UVI's first Ph.D. program" would be the start of a new era for UVI. Up until this point, the University of the Virgin Islands was a Master's level institution, offering an MBA, Master's degrees in Education, Master of Arts in Psychology, a Master in Public Administration, Master in Mathematics for Secondary Teachers, and a Master in Marine and Environmental Science. Any or a collection of these master's level programs could provide the base for a PhD.

UVI had additional strengths that could create the foundation for a PhD program. UVI is a Land Grant institution, with extensive research in Agriculture. Further, the Virgin Islands (through UVI) had $20 million over five years funding from the National Science Foundation's EPSCoR (Experimental Program to Stimulate Competitive Research) program, the third such round of funding. Through this project, UVI had been able to build a world-class research infrastructure for marine science, and other areas relevant to STEM and STEM Education in the Virgin Islands. Funding provides for the hiring and support of active researchers.

Even with building blocks in place, and the commitment of the institution through its strategic plan, administrative leadership was a necessary catalyst for the development of a PhD degree program. As the chief academic leader, I recognized this as a complex challenge that would require an adept approach.

Choosing the right approach to leadership

Malcolm Gladwell's *David and Goliath* (Gladwell, 2013) explores the idea of underdogs who, surprisingly, exceed expectations given conventional reasoning. In many cases, the "Davids" in the examples are able to utilize what may appear to be their weakness in order to succeed. This approach resonates with me. As UVI works to grow competitively, it is clear that its approach to growth will not be the same approaches used by larger, more resourced institutions. A deep understanding of UVI's inner strengths and inner workings was necessary in order to create an authentic program unique to UVI.

Along my continuing leadership journey, I have been most intrigued by the study of creativity. Through various projects in which I have been involved, UVI has forged a relationship with the International Center for Studies in Creativity at Buffalo State University in New York. I have been involved in programs with persons who either studied at the Center, or are faculty at the Center, and through these interactions, have been inspired to read numerous books and articles in the field. This type of thinking encourages us to reframe challenges into questions that may begin with "How might we...?". Focusing on creativity always makes me hopeful that a way forward exists; it just needs to be discovered. Also resonating with the process of fulfilling UVI's strategic plan goals was the concept of *frugal innovation*, which Vavi Radjou spoke about in his 2014 TED talk on *Creative Problem-Solving in the Face of Extreme Limits*. The scarcity of resources can force us toward a more creative idea.

Size, complexity and resource limitation push UVI toward creative approaches. We were preparing to take the big step to being a doctoral granting institution, with the resources of a small, comprehensive, land grant, primarily teaching university. Our first PhD could not merely replicate something that existed elsewhere, but had to be uniquely UVI's.

The process for determining UVI's first PhD program should capitalize on existing and emerging areas for growth. However, because we were charting new territory, I chose to adopt a model of collaborative leadership—recognizing that new and innovative ideas could emerge from where one might least expect. A call for PhD proposals went out to faculty, deans, and directors of centers encouraging the submission of a concept paper outlining the proposed program, the rationale, the targeted audience, and possible partners. Surprisingly, there were no proposals from the university's areas of research strength. Though strong, a focus on PhD development at this time would steer much needed research efforts away toward program development. They opted to have the process and framework developed first by other programs while they continued to strengthen. In parallel, in order to spark creativity, I had brought multidisciplinary groups together to examine the feasibility of two different focuses: Leadership and Creativity; and Sustainability. Both had the potential to be trans-disciplinary (i.e. incorporating the viewpoints and expertise from various disciplines to create a new approach) and impactful in the Virgin Islands territory. Trans-disciplinarity would build on UVI's inner strength of smallness. There was interest in both areas with proposals arising from each. At the end of the process, it was determined that Creative Leadership for Innovation and Change would be UVI's first PhD program.

We soon recognized that partnerships would lead to an innovative program, and bring expertise that did not currently exist at UVI. Fueled by my longstanding relationships and collaboration with innovative and unique graduate programs, the proposal leading to the PhD in Creative Leadership for Innovation and Change was developed. I leveraged existing relationships with Buffalo State's International Center for Studies in Creativity and Fielding Graduate University, where I served on an advisory board. The International Center for Studies in Creativity offered graduate certificates and master's degrees, but none at the doctoral level. Fielding Graduate University offers only graduate education. The Fielding model of delivery informed what would become the UVI model, which aimed to connect with students through one-week residencies that were face to face. UVI built on that approach and made the overall program more personal through offering other synchronous interaction in courses through technology. Buffalo State and Fielding were able to offer areas of specialization for the PhD that UVI could not do on its own. These partnerships also served to expand the faculty base for the PhD program through dual credentialing of students: students would receive graduate certificates from the partner institutions and PhD from UVI. However, working with the Deans of areas with existing master's programs, we developed specialization areas in UVI's School of Education and School of Business. What was clear was that the PhD program, even in its design, would be creative.

The program was also designed as a scholar-practitioner model to meet the needs of the many working professionals in the Virgin Islands who are unable to relocate in order to obtain the PhD degree. Hands-on experiences and action research were inter-woven throughout the program so that the participants might be able to connect the in-class material with their employment positions. This approach was intentional. The leadership program aimed to train leaders in and for various agencies and sectors, with the hope that the program would eventually impact the very core of many governmental and non-governmental agencies in the Virgin Islands. The PhD in Creative Leadership for Innovation and Change sought to transform leadership models in the Virgin Islands.

Transformational Change—making it last

The creation of a PhD needed to be a sustainable change. Thus, separate from the work to develop the academic program, a PhD framework had to be established, which included the requirements for any UVI PhD program. The process was one of exchange of ideas with faculty committees, and the faculty body. Proposals were created by smaller groups and brought to the faculty, who reviewed and debated the finer points. At the end of the process, the faculty was able to adopt a framework that reflected their thoughts and suggestions. This process was often challenging, as there were some who had a philosophical disagreement with the offering of a PhD at that time. An open mind and deep listening skills were important for success. It was important to hear the concerns, and address each one. In particular, the approach taken was to receive the concerns in writing, and then answer each area in depth, with rationale and examples informed by the practices of other institutions. No concern was too small to be addressed, and none were dismissed. After many months of negotiation, faculty overwhelmingly passed the framework. This meant that any program wishing to offer the PhD degree now has a series of expectations clearly articulated in a university policy.

What I learned about leading for campus transformation

Leading initiatives that can transform an institution requires a collaborative approach at every juncture. The creation of the *Pathways to Greatness* strategic plan, which laid out the desired outcome of granting the PhD, was a result of input from across the university. However, it was important for me to recognize that input from across the university is not the equivalent of overwhelming support—especially for institution transformation. And so the implementation required constant negotiation, education, and garnering support, sometimes a person at a time, and often a group at a time. There were many who indicated that the university was not ready for offering a doctoral degree. There was fear that this would take away from what some perceived as the primary focus of the institution—undergraduate education. There was belief that the master's programs were not yet strong enough, and prior to focusing on the PhD, efforts should be focused there. However, there were many who had been at the university through other transformations, and they encouraged me by sharing their stories from other critical junctures in the history of the institution. At the inception of the university in the early to mid-1960s, there were those who thought energies should be focused on the high schools and the Territory was not ready for an institution of higher education. However, the creation of the university has been one of the most transformative actions that the Territory has taken, and a majority of UVI graduates are in the Territory making valuable economic, social and political contributions to the community. This knowledge deepened my belief that the PhD could have a similar impact in the Virgin Islands, and strengthened my resolve to work with faculty to hear their concerns, and then engage a faculty team to work through and address these.

UVI's campus transformation could not exist in a vacuum, or rise out of nothing. Its roots had to be authentically UVI. Building new programs through partnerships was not new to UVI. There were historic partnerships that encouraged UVI students to study for a time at certain universities in the continental US. There were also partnerships that paired UVI degrees with degrees at other institutions. One such leads to a dual degree in Applied Mathematics (from UVI) and Engineering (from partner institutions) after students spent three years at UVI and two at the partner institution. There were also similar degrees that offered a bridge to medical school. The articulation agreements that were created with Buffalo State and Fielding were modeled using these existing partnership agreements. Thus, there was precedent that was steeped in UVI practices, and in a UVI core practice of being a vehicle for providing opportunities to Virgin Islanders.

For transformation to be lasting, policies needed to be created or updated. The creation of the policies for the PhD degree utilized existing master's degree policies and practices governing the most research intensive master's existing at UVI: Master in Marine and Environmental Science. This ensured that existing policies were respected, and provided a touchstone for faculty.

Leading campus transformation requires that you draw on your strengths and experience. While faculty in the Mathematics department, I engaged in what might be referred to as "linchpin leadership". I was involved in the creation of various student programs, and worked with colleagues to study what was done at other institutions to determine what approaches might be appropriate for UVI. In particular, I was instrumental in creating the dual degree for Applied Mathematics and Engineering. Many students would attend UVI for two years and transfer to other institutions for their degrees, thus never becoming UVI alumni. I thought it important that these students have a deeper link to UVI and looked at similar models at other institutions. I also served as a National Science Foundation program officer, where I was able to appreciate the variety of approaches utilized by institutions across the nation. I saw the many collaborations that institutions had, and was and continue to be open to hearing and learning from others. This has resulted in networking opportunities that lead to key partnerships for UVI. Thus, I believe that this important campus transformation initiative took the shape that it did because of what I brought to the project: experience in creating programs, partnership opportunities through networking, and creative thinking that sought solutions that otherwise might not materialize if we focused solely on what was implemented elsewhere.

Epilogue

The UVI PhD in Creative Leadership for Innovation and Change was launched in 2016. This is an intensive three-year, 60 credit program that utilizes Fall, Spring and Summer semesters. In addition to core curriculum and research methods courses, each student completes one specialty track of 18 credits. Specialization in Education and Business can be completed at UVI. The Creativity and Change Leadership track is completed through Buffalo State leading to a graduate certificate. The Human and Organizational Development track is completed through Fielding Graduate University, also leading to a graduate certificate from Fielding.

The first cohort of 50 students started in Fall, 2016. The second cohort of 42 students began in Fall, 2017. At the writing of this article, UVI was preparing for Cohort III.

Students in the program are from the US Virgin Islands, the eastern Caribbean, the continental United States, the Marshall Islands, and Guam. The first graduates will be those that entered having completed the Creativity and Change Leadership track at Buffalo State, and UVI expects to award its first PhD degree in May, 2018.

References

(2018, February 25) Retrieved from https://www.uvi.edu/administration/about-uvi/history.aspx

(2018, February 25) Retrieved from https://www.uvi.edu/files/documents/Board_of_Trustees/Resolutions_and_Actions/2012%20Index%20of%20Resolutions%20and%20Actions/June_2012_08a.pdf

(2018, March 4) Retrieved from https://www.ted.com/talks/navi_radjou_creative_problem_solving_in_the_face_of_extreme_limits

Gladwell, M. (2013). *David and Goliath: Underdogs, misfits, and the art of battling giants* (First edition.). New York: Little, Brown and Company.

CHAPTER 16

Success is O.U.R.S.

Olga Bolden-Tiller, PhD

For years, Historically Black Colleges and Universities (HBCUs) have been known for taking a heterogeneous population of students and turning them into success. Despite the circumstances of these institutions' student populations, the students at HBCUs are well-trained and well-rounded. The opportunity for minority students to be trained in an environment where they can not only be accepted for themselves, but also be celebrated while being themselves has led to a "culture" that many refer to as nurturing when, in fact, it is simply the understanding of needs of HBCU students by individuals who can relate to these students' needs, allowing for their needs to be quickly addressed.

Booker T. Washington (BTW) and George Washington Carver (GWC) were two such individuals who were able to do just this. Although neither man was born in the deep south, the desire to be educated as well as the understanding that southern farmers could benefit from agricultural training drove BTW and GWC, respectively to AL and it was through their efforts as others like them that Tuskegee University (TU) was established and has thrived as the "Pride of the Swift Growing South" serving as an inspiration to many near and far.

TU continues to bring a plethora of individuals, many of whom continue to be underrepresented individuals, either by race, socioeconomic status, etc., together who share common goals and have a common thread. And still today the institution works to provide a strong foundation for students to be well trained. HB-CUs are often credited with doing more with less, which is, unfortunately, becoming a regular expectation throughout education today. For years, institutions, such as TU, have been known to look around them to identify resources to get the job done and although these resources may not have been obvious, they were indeed that. For instance, it is said that when GWC first came to TU to establish an agricultural research program, there were no lab or research materials. Forced to look around to identify resources to get the job done, Carver went out to junk yards to salvage items that could be used as lab equipment for his initial research. Similarly, in 1945, TU established the first and only veterinary school at an HBCU, allowing for the training of African Americans (AA) during a time when few had the opportunity to study veterinary medicine as a result of segregation and other racial barriers (Adams 2004). Over the years the TU School of Veterinary Medicine, now TU College of Veterinary Medicine, has produced over 70% of AA veterinarians as well as the majority of other underrepresented groups, including Latinos, in the United States and continues to be the most diverse veterinary school in the country with ~80% of its students from UnderRepresented Minority (URM) groups (Adams 2004). Despite this success, the field of veterinary medicine remains one of the least diverse fields (Asare 2007).

In 2012, National Science Foundation (NSF) Opportunities for UnderRepresented Scholars (OURS) was established to empower women, especially women of color to aim for higher positions in Higher Education, using an online platform plus two residencies with a special focus on STEM disciplines. To date, the program has been responsible for training almost 50 minority women from minority institutions across the country, including HBCUs, community colleges, tribal colleges and others. And although the time has passed when looking around to identify resources to get the job done means going to the salvage yard, it is still necessary to identify resources to enhance teaching and research as well as extension at land grant institutions, such as TU. Many think it is a mystery that HBCUs are responsible for producing as many as 40% of AA college graduates in STEM fields while only representing ~3% of institutions in the US (National Science Foundation, 2011), often attributing it to "nurturing" versus training of students that actually takes place at these institutions.

However, as a participant in the inaugural cohort of OURS, it became clear that although these institutions are successful in what they do and reports by NSF have demonstrated the true impact of HBCUs, clearly detailing their importance and significance, much of the training at the institutions could benefit by being documented as models that could benefit other institutions (Mack et. al., 2011). The NSF OURS program, with its curricular requirement for an action learning project (ALP), provided an opportunity to develop a model program for the success of the TUSVM, now TUCVM. For years, the veterinary school at TU has partnered with the undergraduate Animal and Veterinary Sciences program in the College of Agriculture, Environment and Nutrition Sciences (CAENS) as a feeder program, with two tracks to veterinary school (Science Option and Veterinary Science Option). With this in mind, I along with Dr. Ruby Perry, then the Assoc. Dean for TUSVM, now the Dean of TUCVM, set out to document the partnership and its success as well as develop and implement enhancements to ensure that students interested in veterinary medicine were well-trained to successfully complete the demands of veterinary school. Specifically, the purpose of my ALP was to develop a structured feeder program at TU for undergraduate students aspiring to become veterinarians, with stakeholders to include students, alumni and potential employers. Although the longstanding partnership between TUCVM and the Department of Agricultural and Environmental Sciences (DAES) within CAENS had been successful, previous efforts were not well documented, had not been optimized and assessments were severely limited.

What went well

The ALP resulted in a number of successes for the PVM Scholars Honors Program as outlined below.

1. An official name was given to the partnership called the Pre-Vet Med (PVM) Scholars Honors Program.

2. A memorandum of understanding (MOU) was signed between CVM and CAENS that included a new opportunity for admission into TUCVM through a process called Early Assurance of Admission.

3. Promotional materials, including a website, were developed to promote the program to prospective and current students.

4. Well-designed PVM Scholars Honors Program guidelines were established, including a handbook, seminars, outline of requisite participation in volunteer program as well as the Pre-Vet Club.

5. The program was presented to stakeholders, including TUCVM Alumni Association.

6. Recently, funding for three years through the United States Department of Agriculture National Institute of Food and Agriculture Capacity Building Program (#2017-07496) was obtained.

Although initially the goal of the program was to establish a program for TU, the funding opportunity was such that the TU PVM program will also serve as a model for another HBCU, Delaware State University, another feeder school for TUCVM, establishing a PVM Scholars Program at that institution.

Positive Impacts At TU

Positive observations resulted from the increased coordination of the collaborative efforts between CAENS and CVM.

1. An increase in the number of TU students matriculating into veterinary school since the inception of the program (~5 years) was noted.

2. An increase in the retention of talented CAENS undergraduates choosing to matriculate at the TUCVM.

3. An increase in number of collaborative efforts between TUCVM and CAENS as well as other institutions for which the PVM Scholars Honors Program may serve as a model, including acquisition of joint grant funding to support said programming and the development and implementation of a Pre-Veterinary Student Symposium hosted by TUCVM.

What the Data Shows

If we take into consideration the TUCVM Class of 2015, of the 70 students admitted, 21 were TU students of which 20 were Animal and Veterinary Science majors, 16 of whom were participants in PVM Scholars activities and represented ~20% of their Freshman class, double the national average for the number of students who enter veterinary school compared to those who express interest in the major during the Freshman year. Of the 21, 17 participated in PVM Scholars activities as outlined above, and

16 out of the 17 of these PVM Scholars successfully completed TUCVM (1 withdrew due to financial issues) compared to only 50% of the students who did not participate in the PVM Scholars program, which was similar to the observations of the number of Tuskegee University Animal and Veterinary Sciences students from CAENS who successfully completed TUCVM in previous years. Although this is a snapshot year, with the recent funding received for the program, next steps will include more detailed assessments of the program through better developed evaluation tools as well as a more thorough analysis of CAENS student success at TUCVM and other veterinary schools. More substantial data on the outcomes, intended and unintended, are expected to be generated as a result in the coming years.

Next Steps

As indicated above, more substantial data on outcomes are expected through the development and implementation of assessment tools that will determine the qualitative and quantitative impacts of the PVM Scholars Honors Program. Thus, the next steps include the following:

1. Optimize assessments for the program.
2. Evaluate PVM Scholars program.

Conclusion

In conclusion, although the PVM Scholars Program was initially piloted using limited resources to get the job done, the NSF OURS ALP served to ensure that this program went forward with all of the steps of an ALP, which resulted in the goals of the program being reached and beyond. Further, the ALP served to facilitate my leadership in showing me the importance of thinking beyond my current position in the academy, to instead consider broader university issues as well as the role of resources and their utilization.

References

Adams, E. W. (2004) "A Historical Overview of African American Veterinarians in the United States: 1889–2000." *Journal of Veterinary Medical Education* 31(4): 409-413.

Asare, A. (2007) "The Attitudes of Minority Junior High and High School Students Toward Veterinary Medicine." *Journal of Veterinary Medical Education* 34(2): 47-50.

Greenhill, L. M. (2009) "Diversity Matters: A Review of the Diversity Initiative of theAssociation of American Veterinary Medical Colleges." *Journal of Veterinary Medical Education* 36(4): 359-362.

Mack, K. M., Rankins, C. M., Winston, C. E. (2011). "Black Women Faculty at Historically Black Colleges and Universities: Perspectives for a National Imperative," in Henry T. Frierson, William F. Tate (ed.) *Beyond Stock Stories and Folktales: African Americans' Paths to STEM Fields (Diversity in Higher Education, Volume 11)* Emerald Group Publishing Limited. 149 – 164.

CHAPTER 17

Transforming Opportunities into Realities: Building a STEM Ph.D. Pipeline at an HBCU
Sherrice V. Allen, PhD

If given an opportunity, I will make it a reality.
I am the author of my own destiny.
Sherrice Allen

Do not follow where the path may lead. Go instead
where there is no path and leave a trail.
Ralph Waldo Emerson

Opportunities in a Barren Land

It seems that I always had a knack for being at the right place at the right time. From the time I started my journey to obtaining my doctorate degree there were amazing opportunities being dropped on my life's path that lead me to where I am today. I cannot imagine not living a life outside of higher education but when I was young I never dreamed of a life in it. Becoming a college professor, a research scientist and an administrator was far beyond my imagination. It was not because I did not have opportunities, but because I did not have the right opportunities nor an awareness that this career path was even possible for an African American young woman. My parents told my siblings and I to pursue a career in medicine due to their exposure. Pursuing a Ph.D. and becoming a professor was never on their radar. Well back in the 70s and 80s there was never a discussion about pursuing a Ph.D., nor was higher education presented as a career option to me. Thus, after graduating from college, I earned a degree in medical technology and worked as a medical technologist in a few local hospitals but I knew there was more. So, after some soul searching I decided to go back to school to obtain a master's degree in biology but I did not know where or what I would do as a career with the degree. During this time, I had moved back home to Fayetteville. Since there was a university in the town with the graduate program of interest to me, it made sense for me to apply. So, I did. It was at Fayetteville State University (FSU) where I began to encounter opportunities in my barren land. My barren land manifested because I lacked the knowledge and exposure to new possibilities such as pursuing a doctoral degree. Also, my mindset at the time made me question my abilities and competitiveness to gain acceptance into a doctoral program and to complete the degree. However, I did not understand the opportunities given to change my barren land were not just for me but also for the many young minority students that I would work with in the future to help change the landscape of their barren lands.

After being accepted into the graduate program at FSU, I met my mentor and provider of countless opportunities. These opportunities laid the foundation upon which I have built my professional life and have allowed me to create a pipeline to the Ph.D. for many minority students. The "opportunity provider" is the title that I have graciously bestowed upon my mentor, Dr. Juliette Bell. Dr. Bell provided me with many firsts in my life. I enrolled in my first graduate course at FSU and she was assigned to teach the course. It was a graduate level genetics course. I was terrified because I had never taken an undergraduate course in this subject but I passed with an "A". She was an awesome teacher and I have patterned my style of teaching after her. The following semester, the opportunities continued and started to change the landscape of my barren land. Dr. Bell asked me to join her on a trip to D.C. to present her research at a national meeting. It was after this experience that I knew I wanted to become a professor and engage in research. The second opportunity came when she asked me to join her research lab to become her first graduate research student. During my tenure in Dr. Bell's lab, there were more opportunities that can be notated as first in my life. I took my first flight to a national conference. I also was one of the first graduates in the M.S. biology program at FSU because of her influence. Finally, I became the first M.S. biology graduate to be accepted in and graduate from a doctoral degree program. It was these opportunities that catapulted me into a career trajectory that made it feasible for me to now be the provider of opportunities to transform the barren land of others.

You may be wondering what all of this has to do with transformative initiatives. Well, I am getting to that. Transformative initiatives do not always start out on a major scale but can begin small. As the old saying goes "Don't despise small or humble beginnings." It is out of small beginnings that major transformative initiatives are birthed. The opportunities that were provided to me in my barren land by Dr. Bell, began to set the stage for my life's work. My task was to build a pipeline for others to follow for undergraduate students or junior faculty. I knew that I had to become poised to assist those who looked like me to transform their own barren lands into flourishing fields of greatness and ample opportunities. I was not fully aware of the task at hand because I had to travel a path that was uncharted by many folks that I knew. I had to become a transformative leader to pursue a dream that was yet unfolding, to forge a trail that would years later be travelled by many leading to the transformation of a university culture.

Leadership is the capacity to translate vision into reality.
Warren Bennis

Without a Vision the People Perish

While matriculating through my doctoral degree program, I was afforded opportunities to increase my capacity to lead. One opportunity came during my last semester of graduate school when I was offered a chance to teach, for a semester, as a lecturer at FSU. The position lasted for a little more than a year but I knew that I needed more training in research and teaching. I needed to complete postdoctoral training. As life had been in the past, I was provided a chance to participate in the first teaching/research post-doc in the country funded by the National Institute of General Medical Sciences (NIGMS), the Seeding Postdoctoral Innovators in Research and Education (SPIRE) Postdoctoral Fellowship Program ("IRACDA Participating Institutions", 2017). Through SPIRE, I became better prepared to pursue a tenure-track faculty position and a vision of my life's work began to blossom. I knew more than ever that somehow, I was supposed to help transform the lives of students at FSU and leave a lasting change at the university. I just did not know how that would unfold or when it would take place. I just knew in my gut that great things awaited me! It was in spring 2002 that an opportunity was provided for me to embark on a journey to become a tenure-track faculty member at FSU. This position opened doors for me to actualize my vision. Often times I wondered if I was equipped to carry out this monumental task of changing the mindsets of students, a campus culture and career trajectory of its STEM graduates.

Prior to joining the department, very few students pursued doctoral degrees. Traditionally biology and chemistry majors, who did pursue an advanced degree, only matriculated into first-professional degree programs (medicine, dentistry, optometry, etc.). Over the years, I heard the dismal statistics regarding the number of underrepresented minorities enrolled in and completing doctoral degree programs in STEM disciplines. Also, I had first-hand knowledge being one of a few minority doctoral students and post-docs in my field at the universities I attended. As a leader, I had to devise a plan to translate my vision into a reality. Oh yes, I had a lot of questions running through my mind. How was I going to manifest the vision that I carried? How was I going to show students that being a research scientist was exciting and a highly rewarding career choice? How would I convince them that they could make it in graduate school? That they could get through the long grueling hours in the lab, the failed experiments and the isolation that underrepresented minorities often face. What tools were at my disposal to begin to prepare them? How could I provide them with time in a research lab when I was just starting my lab? Yes, there were so many questions to be answered but as I would soon learn, I did not have to do it alone. There was a "ram in the bush" available to make my vision a reality. My "ram in the bush" came from the person that provided me with my first opportunity that led me to pursue a doctoral degree, which was the very thing that I wanted to do for the undergraduate students at FSU. It was during fall 2002 that my mentor, Dr. Bell, was awarded a major undergraduate training grant funded through the National Institute of General Medicine at the National Institutes of Health.

The program was the Research Initiative for Scientific Enhancement (RISE) Program, a student centered transformative initiative that I would eventually come to lead. The RISE (R25) program is developmental program that seeks to increase the number of students underrepresented in the biomedical sciences that complete Ph.D. degrees in these fields (RISE program, 2018).

Change starts when someone sees the next step.
William Drayton

Impact Birthed Out of Change

Change is sometimes necessary to move from what has been done to something new and extraordinary. Students at FSU traditionally pursued professional degrees after graduation but a change had come. A change in the campus culture and mindset in regards to what students could do with a degree in biology and chemistry. Through this new initiative, students would be granted opportunities to engage in research, to present their findings at national conferences, to enhance their problem-solving and scientific writing skills and to explore new career tracks. All was made possible through the FSU-RISE program. The framework of the RISE program was based upon the use of well-integrated developmental activities to strengthen students' academic preparation, research training and professional skills (RISE program, 2018). It was this framework that the design of the FSU-RISE program was based upon. The transformation that this single program brought to the university would be long lasting. Due to the campus impact and tremendous outcomes, the FSU-RISE program would serve as the model for the development of other federally funded STEM student enrichment programs on campus as well as at other HBCUs.

In the FSU-RISE program, participants engaged in various academic enrichment and research training activities such as mentoring, academic support, enrichment seminars, biotechnique workshops, research seminars, intramural/extramural training, GRE preparation, and conference participation to prepare them for successful entry into Ph.D. programs. Students also were required to enroll in two courses (Scientific Communication and Molecular Biology courses) to develop their oral and written scientific communication skills and to equip them with the molecular biology research tools and data analysis skills that would be used during their extramural summer research experience as well as in graduate school (Raynor et al., 2014). Although, I did not have the original vision for the FSU-RISE program, yet the intended outcomes of the program aligned with what I desired to accomplish, to create a Ph.D. pipeline at an HBCU.

From 2002 until 2008, I helped to lead this transformation initiative by serving in various positions that include the biotechniques workshop coordinator, a biotechniques workshop facilitator, assistant program director and program director. In addition, I served as an intramural research advisor, mentor, and academic advisor for several program participants. During my leadership with the program, I played an integral role in the development and implementation of key integrated-developmental and research training activities that led to the sustainability of the program. I was able to translate my vision into a reality by helping to create a STEM Ph.D. pipeline at the oldest HBCU in North Carolina. This was a monumental feat. However, as a new leader I was ready for the challenge. Once I became the director of the FSU-RISE program, my mentor had moved on to upper administration and I was totally responsible for sustaining the program and ensuring that our track record of preparing students to matriculate into doctoral degree programs continued. The success of this transformation initiative was clearly on my shoulders. I still pondered if the program was preparing underrepresented minority students to successfully transition into Ph.D. programs. Could the FSU-RISE program continue to serve as a major vehicle for building a Ph.D. pipeline?

According to findings from a 10-year (2002-2010) longitudinal study, the FSU-RISE program was preparing scholars for entry into Ph.D. programs, thus building a STEM Ph.D. pipeline at FSU (Raynor et al., 2014). To determine the impact of the program on transitioning biology and chemistry majors into Ph.D. programs, the study compared which advanced degree programs both RISE scholars and non-RISE scholars entered after graduation, during the pre-RISE (1998-2005) and RISE eras (2006-2013). The pre-RISE era, includes 5-years prior to the implementation of the program and the period when the trend for RISE was being established. During the pre-RISE era, 71% of FSU biology and chemistry students transitioned into professional health programs, 29% of the students entered Master's degree programs and 0% entered Ph.D. programs. However, during the RISE era, 27% of biology and chemistry students entered professional health programs, 43% transitioned into Master's programs, and 30% entered Ph.D. programs (comprised of all FSU-RISE scholars) (Raynor et al., 2014). From 2002-2012, 67 FSU-RISE scholars graduated from the program of which 37 entered advanced degree programs after FSU. Of the 37 scholars, 16 (43%) entered Ph.D. programs, 16 (43%) entered Master's degree programs and 5 (14%) entered a professional health or nursing program (Raynor et al., 2014). In addition, the scholars were better prepared academically, with 85% of the scholars graduating with a grade point average of 3.0 or higher compared to 70% of non-RISE biology and chemistry students.

Thus, the intervention of the program had a transformative impact on both the overall graduation grade point averages and the number of undergraduate underrepresented biology and chemistry students that transition into Ph.D. programs in the biomedical sciences after graduating from FSU (Raynor et al., 2014). A key factor that has allowed the program to flourish was its leadership. As the program director, it was necessary to keep students engaged and abreast about new discoveries in science. In addition, as the director I asked for feedback from at all stakeholders so that decisions made were driven by the data and feedback obtained. During my tenure, several programmatic components were revamped to keep up with the changing research fields supported by the program and to ensure that our graduates were always marketable and prepared to transition to the next level.

Going into its 16th year, the FSU-RISE program continues to be the intervention tool for sustaining a Ph.D. pipeline at FSU. It was a major university transformation initiative that I was given an opportunity to become a major part of and then eventually lead. Through this program, I was afforded a chance to lead an initiative that has transformed the lives of countless students that have earned their Ph.D. and today I now call colleagues. Through this program, students were provided with new career options to pursue. They could transition into doctoral degree programs to become future professors, researchers, administrators, etc. Students would now be able to engage in research and be at the forefront of discovery and innovation. They would be equipped to solve the problems that plagued their families and communities. There is now, an academic intervention and research training program at FSU that would prepare students to transition into doctoral degree programs to obtain the credentials to have a seat at the proverbial table. Just as I had done, when given this opportunity to become equipped to transition into a Ph.D. program, students could make the pursuit of a Ph.D. their reality because they are the authors of their own destiny.

References

Institutional Research and Academic Career Development Award (IRACDA) Participating Institutions. (2017, December 7). Retrieved from https://www.nigms.nih.gov/Training/CareerDev/Pages/PartInstIRACDA.aspx

Research Initiative for Scientific Enhancement (RISE) Program (R25). (2018, February 20).
Retrieved from https://www.nigms.nih.gov/Training/RISE/Pages/default.aspx

Raynor Jr, J. E., Raynor Jr, E., Bell, J. B., Allen, S. V., Whittington, D., Baldwin, C. B., & Naik, A. (2014). Key Practices and Interventions for Training and Transitioning UR Students from an HBCU into Advanced Degree Programs in the Biomedical Sciences. *Atlas Journal of Science Education*, *3*(1), 91-102.

ABOUT THE AUTHORS

Sherrice V. Allen, PhD currently serves as the project director on the North Carolina A&T ADVANCE Institutional (IT) project. She is responsible for the daily management, organization and implement-ation of the project. Prior to joining the project, she served as an independent educational consultant with SVA1 Consulting, LLC, and as the STEM Partnership Coordinator for the North Carolina Center for Afterschool Programs at the Public School Forum of North Carolina. Dr. Allen also has over 15 years of experience as an educator and researcher. For over twelve years, she was on the faculty of the Department of Biological Sciences at Fayetteville State University where she advanced up the ranks from lecturer to a tenured Associate Professor of Biology. Dr. Allen's dedication to excellence in teaching, service and research earned her several departmental and college honors and awards.

Dr. Allen has extensive experience in program management and partnership building. She served as the Co-Principal Investigator for the NIH-funded Research Initiative for Scientific Enhancement (FSU-RISE) grant, serving as the Assistant Director and Director of the program (2005-2008). In addition, she was the Principal Investigator of a National Science Foundation Research Initiation Grant. Finally, she served as the Director of the Center for Promoting STEM Education and Research, (CPSER); funded by Title III (2008 – 2010). As a mentor, teacher and researcher, Dr. Allen is committed to engaging in efforts to diversify the STEM workforce at the undergraduate, graduate and faculty levels.

Dr. Allen received a Bachelor of Science degree in Medical Technology from East Carolina University (1988), a Master of Science degree in Biology at Fayetteville State University (FSU; 1995) and a Doctor of Philosophy degree in Microbiology from North Carolina State University (1999). She completed her postdoctoral training at the UNC-Chapel Hill as part of the inaugural cohort of the SPIRE (Seeding Postdoctoral Innovators in Research and Education) Postdoctoral Research and Teaching Fellows program at UNC-Chapel Hill.

Sandra L. Barnes, PhD is a professor of chemistry and chair of the Department of Chemistry and Physics at Alcorn State University. She received a BS in chemistry (concentration in biochemistry) from Alcorn, a PhD in chemistry (bioanalytical chemistry) from the University of Kansas (KU), and post-doctoral training in pharmaceutical chemistry from KU. She earned a post-graduate certificate in academic leadership from the Chicago School of Professional Psychology through the OURS program. Dr. Barnes' research interest is in analytical method development, particularly in the areas of antioxidant analysis in plants and environmental analysis. She has served on various committees (including IRB chair), published peer-reviewed articles (including a book chapter in an American Chemical Society publication), garnered over $2,000,000 in funding as PI or coPI (from NSF, Thurgood Marshall, USDA, DOD, and MSINBRE), and led efforts to establish the master's degree program in Biotechnology. Dr. Barnes' passion is in providing opportunities for the advancement of undergraduate STEM education, particularly for minorities.

Olga U. Bolden-Tiller, PhD serves as the Head of the Department of Agricultural and Environmental Sciences (DAES) as well as the Assistant Dean of Development for the College of Agriculture, Environment and Nutrition Sciences at Tuskegee University (TU). She holds a BS degree in Agricultural Sciences (Animal Sciences) from Fort Valley State University (1997) and a PhD degree in Animal Sciences (Reproductive Biology) from the University of Missouri- Columbia where she matriculated as an USDA-National Needs Fellow. Following her graduate work, Dr. Bolden-Tiller continued her training at the University of Texas-MD Anderson Cancer Center as an NIH Fellow in Reproductive Biology (2002-2005). In 2005, she joined Tuskegee University as an Assistant Professor and was later promoted to Associate Professor (2012). Since 2008, Dr. Bolden-Tiller has served as the Director for the NSF funded Integrative Biosciences Research Experiences for Undergraduates program at Tuskegee University as well as the Director for summer pre-college programs, including AgriTREK (2011-Present), AgDiscovery (2011-Present), SciTREK (2012-Present), FNR-TREK (2016-Present), Ag Adventure (2014-Present) and DiscoveryTREK (2013-2016).

She is the author/co-author/editor of numerous refereed journal articles, books and conference proceedings. Her research and training programs are funded by the United States Department of

Agriculture; the National Science Foundation; and the state of Alabama (Alabama Agricultural Land Grant Alliance). Collectively, Dr. Bolden-Tiller has served as a research mentor for over 60 high school, graduate (MS and PhD) and undergraduate students. Dr. Bolden-Tiller recently received funding from the Verizon Foundation in support of the Verizon Innovative Learning program which she will direct beginning 2018.

Dr. Bolden-Tiller has received several awards, including the TU College of Agriculture, Environmental and Natural Sciences' Faculty Performance Award for Service (2008, 2017) and Teaching (2010) as well as the Russell Brown Distinguished Scientist Award (2013). Among several administrative and academic fellowships, she was among the inaugural cohort of the NSF/OURS (Opportunities for UnderRepresented Scholars) Fellows which is accompanied by the a PostGraduate Certificate in Academic Leadership awarded by The Chicago School of Professional Psychology (2014) as well as an alumnus of the Lead 21 Program (2014) and in 2016, she completed the 2016 Fielding/Conclave Leadership Academy held in conjunction with the STEM Women of Color Conclave.

Lisa D. Brown, PhD is an Associate Chair and Associate Professor in the Department of Biology at Morgan State University. Dr. Brown earned a B.S. in Microbiology from the University of Rhode Island, M.S. and Ph.D degrees in Physiology from the University of Connecticut, and a Post-Graduate Certificate in Academic Leadership from the Chicago School of Professional Psychology. Her early research interests focused on how neural activity affects muscle plasticity. Studies published from her research demonstrated both morphological changes (T-tubule reorganization in adult muscle fibers and myotube formation from satellite cells) and physiological changes (changes in peak $Ca2+$ transients during stimulation, changes in $Ca2+$ spark production) that correlate with a transition back toward the embryonic state, thus a process indicative of dedifferentiation. More recently, Dr. Brown has shifted from bench work to focus on strategies that promote undergraduate research training and the development of critical thinking skills in STEM-related disciplines. As the Coordinator of the Honors Program within the School of Computer, Mathematical and Natural Sciences, she has developed a series of Honors Interdisciplinary courses that focus on the development of critical thinking skills through writing exercises, analysis of scientific literature, and the development of either a research-based or literature-based thesis. Dr. Brown co-directed the MARC U*STAR Program at MSU from 2009-2014, a program that served to increase the numbers of minorities that pursue advanced degrees in the biomedical sciences by providing undergraduate research training experiences. More recently, Dr. Brown was awarded an NSF HBCU-UP grant to implement an academic program that promotes critical thinking activities, high-impact teaching practices and research experiences that will increase persistence (retention) of students in STEM following the freshmen year. She is also serves as a grant reviewer on the NIH Training and Workforce Development Review Subcommittee C.

Michelle Fletcher Claville, PhD is the Assistant Dean for the School of Science at Hampton University, and a Professor of Chemistry at the University in Hampton, Virginia. She is also the Principal Investigatory and Project Director of *The Nanoscience Project at Hampton University* (NanoHU). Prior to joining Hampton University in 2011, she served as an Associate Professor and Chair in the Department of Chemistry at Southern University and A&M College (Baton Rouge, Louisiana), an Adjunct Associate Professor of Chemistry at Louisiana State University (Baton Rouge, Louisiana), and a Senior Research and Development Chemist at Albemarle Corporation (Baton Rouge, Louisiana). Dr. Claville received the Ph.D. in Chemistry, a B.S. in Chemistry, and a B.A. in English, from the University of Florida, Gainesville, Florida.

Since joining the academy in 2002, Dr. Claville has made gains in scholarship. Dr. Claville is a recipient of the National Science Foundation (NSF) Historically Black Colleges and Universities Undergraduate Program (HBCU-UP), Achieving Competitive Excellence (ACE) Implementation award, and the prestigious NSF Faculty Early Career Development (CAREER) award. With these and numerous other grant awards, Claville has mentored scores of students (high school, undergraduate and graduate students) and a post-doctoral researcher in physical organic chemistry research on biomolecules and nanomaterials. Together with her protégés, she has published the results of her research in a number of scientific publications, and presented at over 50 scientific conferences. One of the more prominent technical meetings is the 2012 *Posters on the Hill* conference (on Capitol Hill, Washington, D.C.), sponsored by the Council for Undergraduate Research. Several of her students have received awards or recognitions at meetings such as, the American Chemical Society (ACS) national conference, National Institute of Sciences/ Beta Kappa Chi (NIS/BKX) joint meeting, Emerging Researchers Network (ERN) and the Annual Biochemical Research and Conference for Minority Students (ABRCMS).

2015, Dr. Claville was invited to present the results of her work with NanoHU at the *Gordon Research Conference on Chemistry Education: Research and Practice* (Lewiston, Maine). Later that year, she was invited to present her work at the annual international meeting of the *Society of Nanoscience and Emerging Technologies* (Montreal, Canada). Dr. Claville is a grant reviewer for the NSF, the ACS, and the Cottrell Foundation. She is currently serving a second term on the ACS's Committee on Professional Training (CPT), the approval body for undergraduate chemistry programs at universities and colleges across the United States.

Kimari Engerman, PhD is the Acting Dean and Associate Professor of Psychology in the College of Liberal Arts and Social Sciences at the University of the Virgin Islands (UVI). She received her Doctor of Philosophy degree in Educational Psychology from Howard University and completed a Postdoc in Engineering Education at the Center for the Advancement of Engineering Education. Dr. Engerman also received a Post-Graduate Certificate in Academic Leadership from the Chicago School of Professional Psychology through the Opportunities for UnderRepresented Scholars which was funded by the National Science Foundation. Also, Dr. Engerman successfully completed the Quality Education for Minorities, Leadership Development Institute. She has served as principal investigator and co-principal investigator on various grants. In addition to serving as the Assistant Director for the Center for the Advancement of STEM Leadership (CASL), she held the following leadership positions at UVI: Provost Fellow; Interim Dean for the College of Liberal Arts and Social Sciences; Chair, Academic Advising Committee; Chair, Dual Credit Committee; Chair, Institutional Review Board; Developer and Coordinator, Junior Faculty Mentoring Program; and Coordinator, Faculty Development Writing Group. Dr. Engerman is the lead editor for *Women Called to Lead*.

Tamara Floyd Smith, PhD is Associate Provost (2017-present) and Professor of Chemical Engineering at Tuskegee University in Tuskegee, AL. She provides leadership on assigned matters in all academic programs at the university. These include 29 academic departments, Graduate Studies and Research, the Library, the Chapel, the Global Office and both regional and discipline specific accreditation matters.

Dr. Floyd Smith, a licensed professional engineer, is a Senior Member of the American Institute of Chemical Engineers (AIChE) and currently serves as a Program Evaluator for ABET, the engineering accrediting body. During her academic career, she secured more than $2.5M in extramural funding as Tuskegee University Principal Investigator, published more than twenty peer reviewed journal publications, was primary advisor for five graduate theses/dissertations and received numerous awards. After twelve years as a productive academician, she was named Interim Assistant Provost shortly after completing requirements for a 16 credit hour, online, Opportunities for Under Represented Scholars (OURS) post-graduate certificate program in academic leadership in April 2015. She was named Assistant Provost in August 2016. She received a fellowship to participate in the Council of Independent Colleges (CIC)/American Academic Leadership Institute (AALI) Senior Leadership Academy in 2017 and was promoted to Associate Provost later that year.

Dr. Floyd Smith completed her B.S. degree in chemical engineering at Tuskegee University in 1996. She went directly to graduate school and earned both an M.S. in chemical engineering practice and a Ph.D. in chemical engineering from MIT in 1998 and 2001, respectively. After completing her graduate studies, she joined Lucent Technologies as a Member of Technical Staff from 2001-2003. Fifteen years ago, in 2003, she joined the faculty of Tuskegee University as an Assistant Professor of Chemical Engineering. She was promoted to Associate Professor in 2007, earned tenure in 2009, was named 3M Scholar (an endowed chair position) in 2009 and was promoted to Full Professor in 2012. She has been married for thirteen years with two children, ages 11 and 5.

Bianca L. Garner, PhD is Interim Provost/Vice President for Academic Affairs and Professor of Biology at Tougaloo College. She received a BS in chemistry from Xavier University of Louisiana, a MS in microbiology from the University of South Florida and a PhD from the University of Mississippi Medical Center. She has been the recipient of more than $1 million in extramural funding for undergraduate support, severing as the co-PI of the National Science Foundation's (NSF) HBCU-UP and S-STEM. She has received several research grants, including a NSF Molecular and Cellular Biology Investigator Initiated Award and the Mississippi National Institutes of Health (NIH) INBRE. Dr. Garner has served as a grant reviewer for NSF and the American Colleges and University's Project Kaleidoscope. She is also a journal reviewer for MDPI Pathogens and Toxins. She is currently a NIH Programs to Increase Diversity Among Individuals Engaged in Health-Related Research Functional and Translational Genomics of Blood Disorders Fellow. Dr. Garner's administrative positions include Assistant Dean and Chair of the Biology Department.

Triscia Wharton Hendrickson, PhD earned a Bachelor of Science degree in Biology from the University of the Virgin Islands (St. Thomas campus) where she was a MARC scholar, followed by a PhD in Biochemistry, Cell and Developmental Biology from Emory University. She completed her post-doctoral training in the Fellowships in Research and Science Teaching (FIRST) program at Emory University School of Medicine, after which she joined the faculty of Morehouse College where she is a tenured Associate Professor in the Biology Department. During her time at the college she has provided leadership in many roles, including as the Director of the MARC-USTAR program, a member of the SACSCOC Reaffirmation of Accreditation Leadership Team, a faculty representative on the Institutional Effectiveness Council, chair of the Faculty Council (2014-2016), and chair of the Faculty Research Committee (2009-2010). She currently serves as the Interim Director of the Office of Research and Sponsored Programs. In addition to her administrative duties, she maintains an active research lab where she investigates the role of Cilia in disease and development and trains undergraduates. Her research has been funded by grants from the National Institutes of Health and private foundations. Dr. Hendrickson is an active member in the scientific community: she has served on the Women in Cell Biology and the Education Committees of the American Society for

Cell Biology, and as a grant reviewer for the National Science
Foundation and the Howard Hughes Medical Institute Undergraduate Program.

Amber B. Hodges, PhD is an Associate Professor in the Department of Psychology at Morgan State University. Her current research examines factors and barriers impacting STEM-efficacy, career aspirations and persistence in minority students. Dr. Hodges was a fellow in the Leadership Development Institute supported by the Quality Education for Minority Network and the National Science Foundation. Additionally, she earned a Post-Graduate Certificate in Academic Leadership from The Chicago School of Professional Psychology through the Opportunities for Underrepresented Scholars Program funded by the National Science Foundation. Dr. Hodges earned her Ph.D. in Psychology from the Graduate School and University Center, The City University of New York (CUNY). She holds an M. Phil in Psychology from the Graduate School and University Center, CUNY, and a B.S. in Psychology from Bennett College. She recently authored a chapter in Women Called to Lead detailing her leadership journey in higher education and has also co-authored a chapter describing successful mentoring models undergirded by psychology theories.

Carolyn Bingham Howard, PhD is a Professor of Biology at Jackson State University (JSU), the urban university in the State of Mississippi. She is trained in the areas of microbiology and pharmacognosy and is the Director of the JSU Breast Cancer Research Laboratory. She is one of the pioneers in the research at JSU geared toward determining the actions/molecular mechanisms of *Vernonia amygdalina's* aqueous leaf extracts (VA extracts) as chemotherapeutic agents to provide a plethora of benefits to patients treated with VA extracts. Her work examining VA extract's efficacy against triple-negative breast cancer (TNBC) cell growth will potentially impact future elimination of health disparities in breast cancer.

Leveraging her background in teaching group exercise and fitness with her research expertise, she hopes to initiate and implement a pilot project program designed to aggressively fight against the obesity epidemic among African-American (AA) girls in Mississippi, while stimulating the emergence of AA health equity researchers. Ultimately, Dr. Howard hopes to help to elucidate a causal link between obesity and breast cancer and is training doctorate-level students in this area of research. She has authored and co-authored several papers on the effects of treatment with VA extracts, displays excellence in teaching and service to JSU, and mentors both graduate and undergraduate research students.

Though a wife, mother of 6 and grandmother of 7, Carolyn Howard served as an NSF-JSU Advance Academic Leadership Fellow assigned to the Dean, College of Science, Engineering and Technology, JSU, a few years ago. During her tenure, she gained first-hand knowledge in problem solving in academia and grasped wonderful, new knowledge useful in her matriculation through the Chicago School of Professional Psychology Post-Graduate Certificate in Academic Leadership Program as an OURS Fellow, and participation in JSU Advance and various STEM Women of Color conclaves. Dr. Carolyn B. Howard feels privileged to have participated in such wonderful programs, life-changing programs. She is a Full Professor and is living, laughing and loving life after OURS.

Cleo Hughes Darden, PhD is the Chairperson and Associate Professor of Biology, a graduate of the Biology Department at Morgan State University (MSU) and participated in the Department's Maximizing Access to Research Careers (MARC) program (1984-1986). She received her doctoral degree from Clark-Atlanta University in Microbial Physiology and Molecular Biology in 1991. Following graduate school, she completed postdoctoral studies at the United States Department of Agriculture (USDA) in Plant Molecular Biology. She joined the Biology Department at MSU in 1993 as an Assistant Professor. Since her initial appointment, she has trained over twenty students in her research laboratory in the areas of Plant Molecular Biology, Cellular, Molecular Biology, and Cell Signaling. She trained NIH and NSF funded students and non-program students who volunteered in her laboratory. Currently, both program and non-program students are in a number of different professions and advanced programs including professional and graduate school, research/laboratory technicians, secondary school teachers, entrepreneurs, and health and science-related fields. In addition, Dr. Hughes Darden served as MARC Program Director at MSU and a total of thirty-five students completed the program; eighty-five percent of these students either completed the PhD or MS degree, are currently enrolled in MS or Ph.D. programs, or are employed in the health and science-related jobs.

Since May of 2013, she has led the Department of Biology as Chairperson and has focused on student success, student research training, instructional delivery improvement, science curriculum through implementation of Vision and Change core concepts and competencies, and faculty development. She actively participated in programs that promote increased student engagement through active learning and the infusion of computation and cultural competency into STEM courses through the Teaching to Increase Diversity and Equity in STEM (Morgan TIDES) program which is an interdisciplinary initiative funded by AAC&U and the Hemsley Foundation. Furthermore, she was appointed both the Coordinator for the LSAMP research program and the Co-Director of the Student Training Core for the full professorship NIH/ASCEND/BUILD program. She served as a reviewer for NIH-NIGMS student training programs and NSF-HBCU-UP programs.

Stephanie Luster-Teasley, PhD is the Professor and Chair of the Department of Civil, Architectural and Environmental Engineering. She joined NCA&T in 2004 after working in private industry as an environmental engineer. Her research specializations include environmental remediation, water sustainability, and engineering education. Over the last ten years, she has been driven by a deep commitment and care for her students and lauded for bringing the excitement of real-world, hands-on experience into all of her engineering courses and mentoring activities.

During her career, Dr. Luster-Teasley has received funding from the Department of Education for developing a mentoring program for students in STEM disciplines, the National Science Foundation for developing and implementing case studies modules in science labs, and the Burroughs Wellcome Fund to implement science programs for middle school girls. Overall, her disciplinary, science education research, and professional development grants have yielded over $7 million in funding.

Camille A. McKayle, PhD is Provost and Vice President of Academic Affairs at the University of the Virgin Islands. Previous to this, she served as Dean of the College of Science and Mathematics.

Dr. McKayle has a deep commitment to quality education. She has served as principal investigator and project director for various grant projects at the university that aimed to strengthen the quality of the preparation in science and mathematics for students at UVI, as well as students in K-12 Virgin Islands schools. The overall goal of those efforts was increasing the number of students that became and remained interested in the Science, Technology, Engineering or Mathematics (STEM) disciplines and ultimately choose to enter into the STEM workforce. The newest project seeks to identify those leadership qualities that have led to the successes that HBCUs have realized in producing quality STEM graduates throughout the years.

From 2005 - 2008, Dr. McKayle was at the National Science Foundation, where she was Program Officer for the Historically Black Colleges and Universities Undergraduate Program, in the Directorate for Education and Human Resources.

Dr. McKayle received her B.S. in Mathematics from Bates College, and M.S. and Ph.D., also in Mathematics, from Lehigh University. Her current research is in the area of STEM Education and STEM Leadership.

Tonya Smith-Jackson, PhD, CPE is the Chair of the Department of Industrial and Systems Engineering at North Carolina Agricultural and Technical State University in Greensboro, NC. She is founder and director of the Human Factors Analytics Laboratory. Tonya earned her graduate degrees from NC State. Her PhD is in Psychology/Ergonomics and her Master of Science is Psychology/Ergonomics and Interdisciplinary Industrial Engineering from NC State. She earned a BA in Psychology from UNC-Chapel Hill. She graduated from the first inaugural class of the North Carolina School of Science and Mathematics in 1982. She spent 14 years at Virginia Tech as a faculty member in Industrial and Systems Engineering.

Tonya's research areas are system safety engineering, cultural ergonomics, and cognitive ergonomics; all of which are applied to various domains using human factors and ergonomics perspectives. She has chaired and co-chaired over 50 doctoral and masters committees since 1999, and served as a member of many committees across STEM disciplines. She is a former associate director of the Center for Innovation in Construction Safety and Health. Her external research has been funded by agencies such as the National Science Foundation, National Institutes of Health, National Institute for Occupational Safety and Health, National Institute of Justice, Office Ergonomics Research Committee, Toshiba Corporation of Japan, Army Research Office, Department of Defense, and United Parcel Service.

Tonya has authored and co-authored over 130 peer-reviewed publications and book chapters. Her recent book, *Cultural Ergonomics: Theory, Methods, and Applications,* focuses on design, analysis, and measurement challenges and solutions when designing systems for diverse users and workers. Her former employment in academia includes the University of Maryland (European Division), City Colleges of Chicago (European Division), NC State University, Wesleyan College, and several community Colleges.

Cheryl A. Swanier, PhD is the Department Chair of Mathematics and Computer Science and an Associate Professor of Computer Science at Claflin University where she is named the Henry N. and Alice Carson Tisdale Endowed Professor. Dr. Swanier conducts research in Human Computer Interaction with an emphasis in visual programming of educational simulations with end user programming and educational gaming technologies. Swanier was selected as a Visiting Research Scientist at Google in Mountain View, California and she received the 2016-17 Google igniteCS Award. Swanier is a recipient of the 2013 NCWIT Undergraduate Research Mentoring Award. Swanier is also the recipient of the 2013 Champion of Change for Tech Inclusion Award given by the White House. She was recognized by Ebony Magazine as one of the 100 Most Influential African Americans in the December-January 2013-14 issue.

Dr. Swanier works with outreach initiatives to improve computer science education at all levels. One of these initiatives is the ARTSI Alliance, Advancing Robotics, Technology for Societal Impact. Another initiative is the STARS (Students & Technology in Academia, Research & Service) Alliance a regional partnerships among academia, industry, K-12 and the community to strengthen local BPC programs by focusing on K-12 outreach, community service, student leadership and computing diversity research.

Dr. Swanier is a member of the NCWIT Academic Alliance and has served as a NCWIT Pacesetter. Swanier provides mentoring to undergraduate students. She facilitates presentations to provide undergraduates with opportunities to gain information on research experiences, internships and on exploring the graduate experience. NCWIT awarded Swanier a $10,000 Seed Fund Award for the *Kewl Girlz Kode* summer learning program during 2016-17.

Dr. Swanier works with many programs focused on increasing the computing pipeline by getting students interested in STEM disciplines and future technology careers. She also conducts outreach activities to organizations such as Girls, Inc., Delta Sigma Theta Sorority, Inc. Delta Academy and Delta GEMS, and Links, Inc. in a concerted effort to broaden participation in computing for underrepresented minorities and girls.

Farrah Jackson Ward, PhD is the Associate Vice Chancellor for Academic Affairs and professor of mathematics at Elizabeth City State University (ECSU). She received her B.S. in mathematics education from North Carolina A&T State University and MS and PhD degrees in mathematics from North Carolina State University. Upon graduation she was a Project NExT fellow and worked as an Assistant Professor in the Department of Mathematics and Statistics at the University of North Carolina Wilmington. In 2007 she joined the faculty at ECSU where she went on to serve as Chair of the Department of Mathematics and Computer Science for 6 years.

Dr. Ward has served as Principal Investigator and Co-PI on several grants from the National Science Foundation and Department of Education. In her current role her responsibilities include overseeing the Division of Student Success, Sponsored Programs and Graduate Education. She has spearheaded several initiatives aimed at improving student success including the implementation of DegreeWorks and the Student Success Collaborative-Campus, a restructuring of ECSU's academic advising services, and a campus-wide reduction in the number of credits required for graduation from 124 – 128 credits to 120 credits. Dr. Ward currently serves on the Executive Committee for the Association for Women in Mathematics (AWM) and has been recognized by EAB for her work on enhancing student success.

About Fielding Graduate University

Fielding Graduate University, headquartered in Santa Barbara, CA, was founded in 1974, and celebrated its 40th anniversary in 2014. Fielding is an accredited, nonprofit leader in blended graduate education, combining face-to-face and online learning. Its curriculum offers quality master's and doctoral degrees for professionals and academics around the world. Fielding's faculty members represent a wide spectrum of scholarship and practice in the fields of educational leadership, human and organizational development, and clinical and media psychology. Fielding's faculty serves as mentors and guides to self-directed students who use their skills and professional experience to become powerful, socially responsible leaders in their communities, workplaces, and society. For more information, please visit Fielding online at www.fielding.edu.

84799029R00149

Made in the USA
San Bernardino, CA
13 August 2018